Internet Banking
and Shopping
for the Older
Generation

Other Books of Interest

BP600   The Internet for the Older Generation

BP601   Computing for the Older Generation

BP602   Digital Photography and Computing for the Older Generation

BP603   Creative Gardening with a Computer for the Older Generation

BP605   How to Find Anything on the Internet for the Older Generation

BP606   Internet Travel and Holidays for the Older Generation

Internet Banking and Shopping for the Older Generation

Greg Chapman

BERNARD BABANI (publishing) LTD
The Grampians
Shepherds Bush Road
London W6 7NF
England

www.babanibooks.com

Please Note

Although every care has been taken with the production of this book to ensure that all information contained herewith is accurate as of the time of writing and that any projects, designs, modifications and/or programs, etc., contained herewith, operate in a correct and safe manner and also that any components specified are normally available in Great Britain, the Publishers and Author do not accept responsibility in any way for the failure (including fault in design) of any project, design, modification or program to work correctly or to cause damage to any equipment that it may be connected to or used in conjunction with, or in respect of any other damage or injury that may be so caused, nor do the Publishers accept responsibility in any way for the failure to obtain specified components.

Notice is also given that if equipment that is still under warranty is modified in any way or used or connected with home-built equipment then the warranty may be void.

© 2004 BERNARD BABANI (publishing) LTD

First published April 2004

British Library Cataloguing in Publication Data

A catalogue record for this book is available from the
British Library

ISBN 0 85934 604 8

Cover Design by Gregor Arthur

Printed and bound in Great Britain by Cox & Wyman Ltd,
Reading, Berks

About this Book

Although there are now many amongst the older generation who have a computer in their home, far fewer feel at ease doing more than simple word processing tasks. This book builds on this level of knowledge, showing that it need not be a daunting task to connect to the Internet and either manage money at an on-line bank or do your shopping.

Some older people, worried about decreasing mobility in the future, may be considering buying a computer specifically for shopping purposes. The book explains how you can experiment with Internet Banking and Shopping without the need to buy a computer. It provides information about the range of goods and services that can be bought on-line – much more than the weekly groceries, books and Compact Discs.

It explains what is needed besides the computer to be able to go Internet Banking and Shopping. This includes how to set up an account with an Internet Service Provider and how to use a web browser. Microsoft's Internet Explorer, the most popular browser, is covered in some depth. There are separate chapters that discuss the important business of keeping appropriate records of transactions, when making on-line purchases. Customisation techniques, including some for those with visual impairments, also merit their own chapter.

Three chapters follow explaining how to use tools such as Web Directories and Search Engines in order to find suppliers of the products or services that those of the older generation may need. A further two chapters cover the entire process of making two different example purchases.

The book concludes with a chapter which aims to settle the nerves of those worried by the scare stories that surround the new world of on-line shopping and appendices that list some sites to explore and describe other facilities available on the Internet besides e-mail and the World Wide Web.

About the Author

Greg Chapman has long had an interest in computers. He applied to transfer to the Westminster Bank's computer department in 1967 when he was working in a branch of the bank in Sussex. However, an early career in computing was not to be and he didn't get to play with a computer properly until 1978, gaining his first computing qualification in 1980.

Since then he has been involved in encouraging the use of computers in many different fields. In the 1980s he was editor of one of the sections of the Sharp Users Club's magazine and managed a "computer camp" holiday project for deprived children. The 1990s saw him installing computer systems and networks in a local authority Emergency Planning office and later working as the Information Systems Training Manager for a County Council's Social Services Department.

After an early retirement in 1998, he began teaching various computing classes for beginners for his local Adult Education service. These include the well-known CLAIT and CLAIT Plus qualifications. He maintains a popular web site, providing help to tutors and students for these courses.

Beyond computing, his interests include boating and the inland waterways of England and Wales.

Greg welcomes feedback about this book at:

http://www.bankandshop.plus.com

Trademarks

Contents

1

A BRIEF INTRODUCTION   **1**
The Aim of the Book   1
What is the Internet?   2
What is a Web Site?   3
How Do I connect to the Internet?   5
Why Shop Electronically?   6
Your Shopping is Delivered to Your Door   7
There's No Need to Leave Home   8
It's Easy to "Shop Around"   8
It's Simple to Find Specialist Suppliers   9
Worries about Internet Shopping   9
Security   9
Complexity   10
Banking on the Internet   11

2

WHAT TO BUY AND WHERE TO BUY IT   **13**
What you can Buy   13
Goods   14
Services   16
Data   17
Where to Buy   19
Traditional Shops   20
Electronic Shops   20
Summary   21

3

WHAT YOU NEED TO GET ON-LINE   23
A Computer Connected to the Internet   23
Your Local Library   24
Cyber Cafés   24
A Suitable Computer for Internet Shopping   26
The Internet Service Provider   27
Dial Up Accounts   28
Broadband Accounts   29
The Modem   30
Dial Up Modems   30
Broadband Modems   33
Internet Connection Costs   35
Dial Up   36
Broadband   37
Summary   38

4

SETTING UP YOUR ISP ACCOUNT   39
Opening an Account with an ISP   39
The General Process   39
Selecting a Username and Password   41
Using an ISP's CD-ROM   43
Using Microsoft's Internet Referral Service   44
Setting up an Account Manually   48
E-Mail Settings   51
Summary   54

5

USING THE BROWSER   55
A Tour round the Browser Window   55
The Menu Bar   55
The Address Bar   56
The Tool Bar   56
The Links Bar   60
The Status Line   61
Working with a Browser   62
Launching Internet Explorer   63
Moving Round a Web Site   64
Moving Round a Page   64
Using Hyperlinks   65
Revisiting Web Pages   68
Back and Forward Buttons   70
History   71
Favorites   72
Links   75
Interacting with a Web Site   76
Summary   78

6

CUSTOMISING THE BROWSER   79
Making Changes   79
Setting the Home Page   79
Setting the History Period   81
Setting Accessibility Options   81
Maximising Screen Space   84
Move and Remove Tool Bars   85
Customize the Toolbar   86
Summary   88

7

KEEPING RECORDS   **89**
If Something Goes Wrong   89
Printing Web Pages   89
Print Preview   90
The Page Setup Dialogue   92
The Print Dialogue   94
Printing Frames   96
The Options Tab   98
Printing Background Colours   100
Screen Dumps   101
Saving Web Pages   102
Summary   103

8

FINDING WHAT YOU WANT   **105**
How to Find What You Want   105
Entering an Address   106
Components of a URL   106
Extended URLs   109
Internet Explorer's Search Facilities   110
Web Searching – Some History   112
Web Searching – Now   115
Summary   115

9

USING A WEB DIRECTORY   **117**
The Web Directory Problem   117
The Yahoo Directory   118
Example Search   122

Google 123
Example Search 125
Conclusion 127

10

USING A SEARCH ENGINE **129**
First Steps 129
The Basic Search 132
Choosing Search Terms 133
Searching for Phrases 134
Avoiding Unwanted Results 135
Searching for Alternative Terms 136
The Advanced Search 136
The Results List 145
Additional Features of the Results List 150
Summary 151

11

THE BANKING PROCESS **153**
From High Street to Internet 153
Banking On-line 154
Logging on 155
Account Lists and Details 157
Statements 160
Transfers 163
Payments 165
Management 167
Applications 168
Summary 169

12

THE BUYING PROCESS   **171**
From High Street to Internet   171
Browsing and Window Shopping   173
Web Site Reviews   174
Asking on Newsgroups   175
Example - Buying more Memory   177
Find the Site   177
Terms and Conditions   178
General Support   178
Select the Product   179
The Checkout Process   180
Example - Buying a Camera   186
Searching for Information   186
The Purchase   188
Selecting Extras   189
The Checkout   191
Summary   196

13

WORRIES   **199**
Buying On-Line   199
Site Worries   199
Before Buying   199
Is it Based in the UK?   200
Do you Want to Buy from Overseas?   200
Will your Data be Shared?   201
What about "The Small Print"?   202
While Buying   203
Use a Credit Card   204

Keep Records   204
After Buying   204
When Complaining   205
Technical Worries   205
Your Computer   206
The Need for a Firewall   206
The Virus Menace   207
A Computer Crash   207
The Site   208
Summary   209

APPENDIX 1

SUGGESTED SITES   **211**
Before you get On-Line: 211
Search Tools: 211
Shops, Stores and Supermarkets: 212
Banks and Building Societies: 213
Miscellaneous: 213

APPENDIX 2

OTHER INTERNET SERVICES   **215**
Usenet/Newsgroups   215
Mail Lists   217
Chat Rooms   217
Other Services   218

INDEX

INDEX   **219**

A Brief Introduction

The Aim of the Book

Our grandchildren may find the Internet as straightforward as programming the video recorder, but for many it's just one piece of technology too far! This book aims to help those who may be happy enough to use their computer to type a letter, but for whom the Internet is rather more intimidating. More specifically, this book should give you the confidence to use the Internet to buy goods and services and complete bank account transactions using a computer.

You may be getting to the stage where getting into town to do your shopping is becoming more difficult for you. Maybe, with the tighter budget that being a pensioner implies, you need to keep a closer eye on your finances, and even a monthly bank statement is not frequent enough. You have a computer. You've seen the adverts on the television. You know that your computer can help, but you're a little worried that it will all be too complicated.

If all this rings any bells, then this book should be for you. If you can get by writing a letter on your computer, you can certainly master internet banking and shopping. In fact, you don't even need your own computer, as will be explained in Chapter Three.

Internet shopping is really nothing more than good old-fashioned mail order! The only difference is that you place an order through a web site, rather than by mail or telephone.

Internet banking is much the same. You use a web site to order transfers between accounts, make payments, or to set up standing orders and direct debits. Unlike telephone banking you have the advantage of also being able to print out your statements and records of your transactions and even get electronic versions which can be imported into your spreadsheet or accounting software, so you do not need to retype it, with the opportunity for errors that offers. It's certainly a lot more comfortable than doing the same thing while standing in the rain, tapping away on the keypad of a bank's cash machine.

What is the Internet?

Many people are confused because, these days, the term "Internet" is often used rather loosely. Many speak of the "Internet" when more correctly they mean the "World Wide Web".

Technically, the "Internet" should refer only to the many computers around the world that are connected one to another, each able to exchange information with any other connected computer. The Internet works in exactly the same way as the modern telephone system. In many ways, the Internet and the telephone system have already effectively merged. These days the telephone system doesn't just handle voice calls, but takes other traffic, such as faxes, as well. Most people's home computers link to the Internet via the ordinary telephone system. In the same way that the telephone system can handle a variety of traffic, computers connected to the Internet can also transmit different types of data along the cables, microwave and radio links that join the computers together.

The two most widely used services available on the Internet are "e-mail" and the "world wide web". If e-mail is the electronic equivalent of posting a letter, then "the web" is the electronic equivalent of publishing. In the context of electronic shopping, it is used as the company's shop window, or perhaps more accurately, a web site will be the equivalent of a mail order catalogue.

Any person or company can put together a web site, for any purpose, but this book will concern itself only with sites that offer goods or services for sale and the various features you are likely to find on them. However, everything you read here is easily applicable to other uses of the World Wide Web, so it should form a good general introduction to the web as well.

What is a Web Site?

A web site is a collection of computer files, known as pages, created by a single organisation. These are viewed in a computer program called a browser.

Internet
Explorer

The most popular browser is Internet Explorer, which comes as part of Windows, the operating system[*] that most computers use. Chapter Five describes how to use Internet Explorer and provides tips for getting the best out of it.

---

[*] An operating system is the special computer program that allows all the different components of the computer system, keyboard, screen, printer, etc., to talk to each other.

Unlike a book or magazine, a web site's pages are not arranged in a fixed order. Instead one moves from one page to another by using "hyperlinks", specially highlighted text or pictures, which may appear anywhere on the page and link the page currently being viewed, with another.

The Saga Home page - just a large menu, with every item a link to another page or section of the site

Selecting a link gets the browser to request that the linked page is sent to your computer from the one on which it is stored. This process requires that the computer is "on-line", i.e. connected to the Internet. As you will request new pages frequently, you will need to be connected all the time you are browsing the web.

Another difference when comparing a book's pages with those of a web site is that they are not necessarily self-contained. Many web sites have links to pages that are on other sites. This saves an original site's author from having to duplicate information and is where the "web" gets its name, as the range of links criss-crossing from one site to another are like the many filaments that compose some types of spider's webs.

Most people using the web will jump from site to site following links that are of interest to them, rather than staying on a single author's site. However, the kind of web sites with which this book concerns itself, those that concentrate on trying to sell you something, are less likely to have external links. They won't want to lose you to a rival supplier!

In order to catch your interest, commercial web sites are frequently constructed with many "small-ads" on their "home page", the page on the site that is intended as the starting point for any visit. These form links to other pages on the site offering more details about their leading products or services. Frequently, these links are duplicated in a set of, often text-based, links arranged as a menu. Such a menu, usually found across the top or down the left-hand side of the page, will normally be repeated on every page, allowing the visitor to navigate around the site easily.

How Do I connect to the Internet?

You need two things, besides your computer, to connect to the Internet, a modem, or an equivalent device if you are connected via "broadband", and an account with an Internet Service Provider (ISP).

A modem is a small piece of equipment, which is normally built into the computer, though machines built before 1998 may not have one fitted. It's the device that changes (modulates) "computer signals" into sound that is sent down a telephone line, or takes incoming sound from a telephone line and changes (demodulates) it back into computer signals.

The name "modem" is made up from the initial letters of each word, MO(dulate) and DEM(odulate). It produces exactly the same kind of squawking noise that you hear if you pick up the phone while a fax machine is running. A little more about modems is explained in Chapter Three.

Broadband is a system that allows much faster transfer of data from the Internet to your computer than is possible through a modem. The extra speed benefits those who use the Internet to watch television or films, or who want to listen to high quality audio broadcasts. Broadband is normally an "always-on" system, which means that if you keep your computer running all the time, you'll be able to hear or see when an e-mail arrives in exactly the same way as you hear the telephone ring. It also makes it practical for you to send large volumes of data. With broadband you can broadcast your own home movies on the World Wide Web and the day of the practical videophone is finally here.

An Internet Service Provider is an organisation that has a permanent connection to the Internet and a bank of modems that allow its customers' computers to connect to it and hence the Internet. When you set up an account with an ISP, besides the ability to browse web sites, you will normally get one or more e-mail addresses, the use of some hard disc space at the ISP, where you can create your own web site and, usually, a number of other services too. Exactly what is provided will vary from provider to provider and from package to package with that provider. Again, there is more about this in Chapter Three.

Why Shop Electronically?

So what is the point of shopping through the Internet when we've all got along perfectly well without it all these years?

Your Shopping is Delivered to Your Door

If you remember, as I do, when milk was delivered on a horse-drawn cart, and different lorries came every week offering greengroceries, fizzy drinks, ice-cream and other goods. If you remember how every few months the man called to service the vacuum cleaner, or another called with a large suitcase, selling all manner of cleaning materials, then you may think how much easier it was when things were delivered.

Tesco: Just one supermarket that will deliver much more than groceries. The home page has menus across the top and to the left of the screen, in an arrangement typical of many sites

In those days you didn't always need to get to the shops. You didn't struggle to find a parking space close to where you needed to be. You didn't have to wait for a bus that didn't come. You didn't struggle with a shopping trolley that wouldn't go in a straight line. You didn't wait forever for the supervisor to arrive to assist the ill-trained youth on the checkout. Wasn't it simple when everything was delivered? The next chapter discusses the range of things that you might want to consider buying on-line and have delivered. Not everything has to arrive in the post. Some things, recorded music for example, can be delivered straight down your telephone line!

There's No Need to Leave Home

Generally, with a few exceptions, Internet Shopping is simply mail order, with the advantage that you don't have to go to the post box to send the order. Neither is there a stamp to be found, nor any need for a trip to the Post Office. It's better than telephoning too, as reputable electronic shops will present you with options to enable you able to generate a printed copy of your order, which can be used as evidence or to refer to if anything goes wrong.

It's more flexible than ordinary mail order too! You can place an order at any time of day or night and you know that the company will be able to work on it immediately, with no postal delays or wait while your cheque is cleared.

It's Easy to "Shop Around"

How often have you been advised to "shop around"? When did you last try an exhaustive look for the best price for something in which you were interested, yet wasn't being advertised in the press? How much did you save after you took account of the telephone and travel costs? Most people give up after checking only a couple of places. However, when shopping via the web it can be a matter of moments to check a range of suppliers for the best deal. In some cases, you will be directly interrogating the supplier's own stock records, so you will not be persuaded into placing an order for something that cannot be dispatched immediately.

Chapter Two will provide information about where to go shopping. Apart from many of the famous High Street names, you'll be introduced to some shops that only exist on the Internet. Further ideas for where to look for goods and services are provided in Appendix 1.

It's Simple to Find Specialist Suppliers

Chapters Eight to Ten will help you find the shops that stock those rare items for that unusual hobby that you pursue, or find suppliers of specialist equipment that is not available in your home town. These chapters offers some useful techniques for using "Web Directories" and "Search Engines" which will help you find sites with information of interest to you, from amongst the millions of web sites out there.

Worries about Internet Shopping

You would not be alone if you were worried about your first Internet purchase. Most newcomers are concerned about two areas, security and complexity. This book concludes with a chapter that provides more advice about dealing with things that go wrong, but let's put your mind at rest before going further.

Security

Often those who express concerns about providing credit card details over the Internet exhibit such bad habits elsewhere that they may, in fact, be safer shopping "on the net". For example, many restaurant customers quite happily give their credit card to a waiter and let them take it away from the table. A number of shops still use mechanical devices to swipe the card and will need to phone the card company to gain authorisation for the transaction.

Any restaurant or shop that does not have its electronic card reader or telephone within sight of the dining area or on the counter is presenting its staff with the opportunity to swipe customers' cards through a reader and so extract their personal data. That data can then be stored and used to make one or more duplicate cards. If you do eat or shop at places that require staff to take a credit card out of view of the customer, then you are considerably more likely to be the victim of a credit card fraud than you are buying through a "secure site" on the Internet.

> **The Secure Connection symbol, found on the status line of your browser, indicating that all traffic to the site from the current page is encrypted:**

Complexity

It is true that your first purchase at many on-line shops will appear complex. In most cases this is because you are not just placing an order and providing a delivery address and payment details. In effect, you are opening an account with that shop and, in the same way that a trader would expect to be asked questions about credit-worthiness when opening an account with a wholesaler, the on-line store will want to know a little about you and establish a secure ordering system, with passwords or account numbers, so no one can impersonate you.

This is important, not only to protect your payment arrangements but also because one of the main ways that an on-line store keeps its costs down is by obtaining and keeping far more detailed records about its customers than the ordinary High Street shop. With these improved records it becomes easier to predict what customers in general are likely to buy, and so enable the store to hold optimum stock levels, and also help predict your individual shopping pattern, so helping the on-line store to provide offers which are likely to be more appealing to you or suggest purchases that you may not have considered.

Wouldn't you like to return to the days of personal service, when your shopkeeper knew that you normally bought a bottle of ketchup every six weeks, and asks if you need one this week? If you regularly order your groceries through the same site, then you are likely to be reminded to make this kind of repeat purchase.

Like any good old-fashioned store offering personal service, though appearing to be somewhat more intrusive initially, it helps the shop offer a better, more personal, service for you during later visits.

Banking on the Internet

Banking on the Internet works in much the same way as internet shopping. It is all done through the bank's web site. As you might expect, the level of security on a bank's web sites is typically higher than that of ordinary on-line shops. Normally, you only gain access to your personal information after entering randomly selected characters from your password or PIN, so that someone has to see you entering this data several times before they could determine your complete password.

Apart from the additional security provided by the web site, you manage your accounts in much the same way as you do with the more sophisticated cash machines or through a telephone-banking service. You can transfer money between your various current and savings accounts, manage standing orders and direct debits, pay your regular household bills, make one-off payments, view and print statements and lists of standing orders or direct debits.

NatWest's OnLine Banking site has a multi-step logon process starting with a "Customer Number" that has nothing to do with any other account numbers or PINs you may use

You can also be sent the information that appears on your statements in a form that can be imported into a spreadsheet or other financial program. This will save you time and cuts out one possibility of error when reconciling your bank statements with your own financial records.

In addition, most banks allow you to apply for different kinds of insurance, order foreign currency, order cheque or paying-in books. In other words, on-line banking will do almost everything for you, apart from deliver you cash.

What to Buy and Where to Buy it

What you can Buy

If you remember the "Light Programme" then you probably recall that old parlour game, "Twenty Questions". The panel had to identify a mystery object by asking just 20 questions that could be answered by either "Yes" or "No". The trick was that the answer "Yes" meant the question wasn't counted, so really the programme should have been called "Twenty No's"! If you do remember it, you'll recall that many people also played the game at home as "Animal, Vegetable or Mineral", because after the "Mystery Voice" had revealed the solution to the audience, the question master would give the panel a clue by announcing that the current object was one of those three things, or occasionally the object would be "Abstract – with animal connections" or some other connection!

In the same way, most people would classify the things that you can buy as either goods or services. But in the on-line world of electronic shopping, it is probably useful to add a third category, "data".

Obviously any goods you buy will need to be packed up and sent to you. This kind of internet shopping is nothing more than mail order with a new way of ordering. Buying services on-line is the same. There's nothing magic about on-line shopping. The only thing that is new is the mechanism for placing the order. Buying data on-line, however, is quite distinct. "Abstract with computing connections", perhaps! Data can be passed down a telephone line. It can, therefore, be delivered to you immediately, as you make your purchase. There is no delay in delivery!

Goods

I have heard it suggested that certain things are not suitable for purchase on-line. Clothes were mentioned as a particular example. It was suggested that clothes are too personal an item. It's so important to ensure a good fit, to be able to touch and feel the fabric and to check the quality of workmanship. Accordingly, it is argued that it wouldn't be sensible to buy clothes on-line. Those who take this point of view contrast buying things such as music CDs or books, where you know exactly what to expect and only damage in transit can occur to disappoint you.

Surely, these people can't have forgotten the days when you would find catalogues from Littlewoods, Grattan, Brian Mills and others in almost a third of the homes in the country, and that the majority of the wares in those catalogues were clothes! It's true that those businesses did begin to struggle in the 1970s with the rise of the credit card. The new form of credit meant that catalogue shopping lost some of its extended credit and "easy payments" appeal, but that was not the key factor for most customers.

The catalogue companies recovered and clothes remain an important part of mail order shopping simply because many people prefer to try things on at home. Shopping for clothes on-line provides exactly that facility. The idea of stripping-off in communal changing rooms is a horror for many older people, and young ones as well, if they don't happen to have a model-perfect shape! All that is needed to make on-line clothes shopping a real joy is the confidence that you can return goods that don't fit and that you will get your refund promptly.

For many, on-line shopping stands or falls according to the confidence that they have that their purchase will be delivered, will live up to expectations and, if it doesn't, that they will get a refund without undue bother. It comes down to choosing a shop you trust – and that need not be a problem since many of the ordinary High Street retailers from whom you have been buying over many years do now offer an on-line service.

With that in mind it becomes easy to think of on-line shops to visit. No longer do you need to "window shop". Now you can just go "browsing". Appendix 1 includes a list of well-known shops that you will find in your local High Street or Retail Park. You can take a look at their web sites and see what they have to offer. If your personal favourite is not listed then the techniques you'll learn in Chapters Eight to Ten will solve that problem.

A number of these shops offer distinct advantages for customers who shop on-line. It is easy to understand why. If customers buy direct, then they don't need so much display and storage space in their shops and there's room for a wider range of goods there, and so encourage more customers. Depending on the goods involved, either dropping off the order while on the way from the warehouse to the shop will save the company money, or because of bulk purchase of parcel delivery services, the additional delivery cost is minimal.

Services

If you can order something on the telephone, then it is certain that you can buy it on-line. Many would argue that it is better to buy on-line than to risk being misheard or not get instant written confirmation of the order to be processed. Take flowers, for example.

For many years the Interflora network has provided its customers with the ability to deliver fresh flowers to almost any address in the world without the flowers having to be moved more than a few miles or the buyer having to worry about the technical details of how flowers get there. It doesn't really matter if you think of the process as one of buying a delivery service, or the purchase of flowers. Now you can do it on-line, as you can when buying made-to-measure curtains or almost anything else that involves goods being finished to your specification.

These days, there is little excuse for handling financial services in any way other than on-line. These are exclusively information-based and there is virtually no physical process involved. Money is, after all, no more than a token of value, originally represented by gold, then by coin, then bank notes, or cheques, and more recently plastic. Since the development of notes a few centuries ago, money has not really been related to anything physical, only being backed by our trust in the ink on a ledger or, more recently, a magnetic anomaly on a hard disc on some computer somewhere. Financial information, therefore, is the perfect subject for on-line dealing, as it involves no more than moving the data around.

Insurance is a case in point. You provide information about yourself, your home, its contents, or your car, for example, and the company promises to pay you if you provide the evidence that a certain set of circumstances has occurred. The conventional insurance proposal form becomes an electronic form on a web page. In fact, buying services can often be thought of as the opposite way round to buying goods. Rather than receiving something, the purchase involves sending the necessary information to the provider of the service.

Sometimes, the reverse applies and the essence of the contract is that you will be provided with information. Information is data, and here we cross into this rather different purchase type.

Data

What is data? In this context it is anything that can be transmitted, or to use the jargon, "downloaded" to your computer, over the telephone line.

Perhaps the most obvious piece of commercial data is the verifiable record that you have paid some money to a company. The last time you took a train journey, went to the theatre or on holiday, all you got to show for your purchase was a ticket. If you, the customer, can obtain the ticket without the need for the provider to maintain large centrally placed office space, then it will save costs. This is precisely why so many companies, these days, encourage on-line purchase, as it saves them costs, which they can pass on to you as reduced prices. The ticket is there to demonstrate your right to avail yourself of the service.

Whilst some services require that you go somewhere to take advantage of them, others, gardening, painting and decorating, home helps and so on, require that someone comes to you. In these cases, the ticket is barely needed at all, unless something goes wrong and you need it as evidence that you have paid. Whatever the service, there is no difficulty, for someone who buys on-line, to print the information that appears on the ticket for themselves.

Even something you may think of as goods, computer software, for example, should be thought of as data. It's true that when you buy software from a High Street shop, you get a cardboard box with a CD-ROM inside. Goods! You then insert that CD-ROM into your machine and "install" the software, that is you copy and integrate the data with that already on your hard disc.

Buying on-line you just do it the other way round. You download it directly to your hard disc, where you then integrate it with your existing data, and then create your own copy on CD-ROM, using your CD writer. As it is increasingly the habit of software producers not to provide printed manuals, there is little point in having a shop-bought boxed version of the software. Not only do you get it instantly, delivered to where you need it, you are guaranteed the latest version, as there is no such thing as old stock, and costs are dramatically reduced, as the costs of distribution are effectively non-existent.

The same goes for music. Since the arrival of the CD, recorded music has been digital, and it has posed big problems for copyright holders. The problem is the ease with which recorded music can be transmitted over the Internet. In particular, the advent of a format for audio files, called MP3, has meant that files have become small enough for it to be practical to download these files, even on slow dial-up connections. Certainly, those in the pop music field are already claiming that the CD is obsolete as a medium for recorded music, so ubiquitous has the MP3 become. The "Walkman", the CD-based personal hi-fi player, is, indeed a largely obsolete product. Now one buys an MP3 player. No disk or tape is involved. The MP3 file is transferred, electronically, into the digital memory of the player and the days of having to worry about jogging the player has gone. However, the market for MP3 files remains very much aimed at the young, and for the immediate future there may be little that middle-aged and older people will find to enjoy.

Technically, there is little to separate video from audio. However, video files are considerably bigger. It required the development of the DVD format, which has a storage capacity several times bigger than a CD, to make video on disk viable. Even on a broadband connection, the size of the files would mean a download lasting a significant period. Copyright issues, too, remain a concern. When the DVD standard was fixed a concession was made to film producers, which enabled a regional coding system to be introduced. This was intended to help film producers reduce the risk of moving DVDs around the world in advance of a film's cinema release locally, and so prevent them losing the box-office revenue. In the immediate future, buying a major Hollywood film on-line will remain as the mail order of a disk, rather than the download of a file. If you do buy a DVD on-line, then take note of the advice about buying from overseas, in the final chapter.

Where to Buy

On-line shopping has matured since the "Dot Com" crash at the end of the 1990s. Many of the companies that survived continue to have only an on-line presence but have still become some of the best-known retailers in their field.

Indeed, it is not just some of the on-line retailers that now have a reputation for reliability or quality of service, but now a number of auction houses are reaching a similar standing and are becoming the favoured place, for many, both to obtain bargains and sell unwanted goods.

Traditional Shops

If you are cautious, and thinking of shopping on-line for the first time, why not turn to a shop you already trust. For most, that could well be one of the ordinary High Street multiples. We all have our favourites. It may be Marks and Spencer, Laura Ashley, John Lewis or Argos. Each of these offers goods for home delivery and purchase on-line. Many others offer the same kind of service. Pick your favourite. If the worst happens, you can pop into town and make your complaint there, in person. Perhaps groceries would be a better starting point. Tesco, Sainsbury, Iceland, and others all offer home delivery services, following on-line ordering. A list of the addresses of some of these shops appears in Appendix 1.

Electronic Shops

Anyone who buys books regularly will have heard of "Amazon", now the largest UK retailer of books. LastMinute's growth was constantly reported during the growth of the "dot com" bubble. It survived the crash and, for many, is the first place to turn to for a cheap holiday break. Those that read the financial press will be aware of that new breed of bank with strange names like "Egg" or "Cahoots". All tend to offer better rates than conventional banks with High Street premises to maintain. eBay is another of the "dot com" companies and, perhaps, the best-known auction site on the net, where anyone can put unwanted goods up for sale.

The point is that almost anything, these days, is available on-line.   Buying on-line can be quick, convenient and certainly is no less reliable than conventional shopping and banking.   Of course some horror stories about on-line shopping and banking are true, but don't forget that "That's Life" used to report just the same kind of thing years before any of us had dreamed of having our own computer, let alone being on-line!   None of those stories stopped us shopping, did it?   Nor should the reports you might hear now on TV and radio consumer programmes like "Watchdog" and "You and Yours".

Summary

There is virtually nothing, goods or services, that you cannot buy on-line.   Banking and other financial services are almost always cheaper and more efficient when handled on-line.   Data is also definitely better bought on-line, as you can be guaranteed the very latest available, virtually instantly.

Most of the conventional high-street shops and nationally known companies that you are used to buying from are waiting to do business with you on-line.   As well as them there are others, which only sell via the web, that are developing a reputation for service the equal of any conventional shop.

Providing you take the same precautions that you would with any mail order house, there is no reason for putting off going on-line to do your shopping.

2 What to Buy and Where

3

What You Need To Get On-Line

A Computer Connected to the Internet

If you are reading this book then you probably already have a computer at home, but you'll need more than the computer itself if you are to go banking or shopping on the Internet. You also need an account with an Internet Service Provider (ISP) and a modem, or its broadband equivalent. If you haven't got both those yet, you can still give the Internet a go, but not at home! The local library will almost certainly have a public access computer that is connected to the Internet and that you can use without charge! You may also live in a town with one or more cyber cafés.

Obviously, for regular use there is no substitute to having your own computer set up and ready to go on-line, but if you're still at the "investigating" stage, then a practice session could be a worthwhile experience. Book a session on a public access computer at your local library or ask if you can have a go when next with your son or daughter or a friend who's already on-line. But before you book or beg that session, finish this chapter and read through Chapter Five.

Once on-line, set yourself the task of finding out if broadband is available in your area, to see if one of the options for connecting to the Internet is available to you at home. Get a feel for things by looking at some web sites that review different Internet Service Providers, check out current prices, or see which are the best modems to buy. Some helpful addresses to use are provided in Appendix 1.

Your Local Library

As the Internet is such a mine of information, and providing information is one of your local library's main functions, most, these days, have a number of public access internet-connected computers ready for their registered borrowers to use. Generally, there is a booking system, allowing half an hour for you to complete your business. However, if no one has booked the following slot, frequently you will be allowed to continue using the computer until someone else requests its use.

The only charge that your local library is likely to make is if you require a printout and you are likely to want one of those if you place an order for some goods and have been presented with a page that confirms the order and quotes an order reference number or despatch date for your goods. Most libraries charge only a nominal sum for this, equivalent to that which they make for making a photocopy, but do check about arrangements for this before you start your internet session.

Cyber Cafés

Apart from libraries, many towns now also have a "Cyber Café". Some of these are commercial ventures, operating in the High Street, and you will have to pay a commercial rate for their use. Many, however, are part of schemes funded by the local council or other public bodies, aimed at improving the education and employment opportunities for the people in their area. These community cyber cafés usually specialise in offering computer training for local people, but many also run free public access sessions for people living within their catchment area, and are only likely to charge a very modest fee if you come from outside their area.

Although the first cyber cafés did indeed start out as coffee shops with the added service of providing internet connected computers to their customers, the term is often used now for any venue that provides a public access internet connected computer and you may find them as additional services at hotels, print shops and conference centres.

Even if you have your own computer, don't forget that cyber cafés are appearing all over the world. It may be worthwhile exploring one in this country before you go on holiday. Then, if you are on holiday and realise that you have forgotten someone's birthday, there'll be less to put you off dropping into one at your holiday destination and arranging to send them a gift, especially if their local shop could deliver it and avoid any postal delays!

Entering a cyber café for the first time can be intimidating. The larger commercial venues can have hundreds of computers available, with credits purchased through a vending machine. The receipt will provide a code, which is entered at the computer to provide the appropriate access time. Rates can vary enormously. In mid-2003, one large London based venue was charging £1.50 per hour at a busy time. Some cyber cafés will offer the equivalent of a bus or train "rover" ticket, with unlimited use allowed during an unpopular time, such as the weekend.

A Suitable Computer for Internet Shopping

Because your internet-savvy grandchildren may be constantly trying to persuade their parents to upgrade their computer, does not mean that the Internet requires a powerful modern computer. Some are surprised that it is games software that is usually the most demanding software installed on a computer, and that straightforward internet banking and shopping is a low-demand task.

People have been on-line shopping for some years and nothing has changed in the basic requirements of the computer. Whilst it may be nice to have the latest technology, almost certainly, you can happily make your purchases using a grandchild's cast-off machine!

Any machine capable of running Windows 98, or a later version of the operating system software, will be good enough for internet shopping. It is very likely that an older machine could be made to work satisfactorily too. However, as I write, Windows 98 is about to be dropped from the list of operating systems still supported by Microsoft. That means that only later versions will be updated, should flaws in the software be uncovered. The flaws to be concerned about here are those that allow "attacks" by hackers whilst you are connected to the Internet. This issue is discussed further in the final chapter.

Anything more recent than Windows 98 is a bonus. It will mean that you have a machine capable of running more powerful non-internet software, and will be more than up to the job of internet shopping.

The Internet Service Provider

If your computer is suitable, the next thing to consider is the kind of connection that you require with an ISP. This decision, if a choice is indeed available, determines the kind of modem you require to link your computer to your ISP. An increasing number of people have the choice of selecting a traditional "Dial Up" or the newer "Broadband" service. Apart from the technical issues, your decision may also be dependent on costs of the different services. Costs are discussed later in this chapter.

When Windows 98 was released, before Broadband became available, it was the habit of many computer suppliers to add icons to the desktop of their newly delivered computers, that you could use to connect, using the computer's internal modem, to an ISP and set up an account. This was especially true in Britain because, as standard from Microsoft, Windows only came with icons for companies that operated in America. With the release of Windows XP, and into the Broadband age, the desktop icons have been replaced with lists of country specific ISPs accessed through the New Connection Wizard and described in more detail in the next chapter.

A second approach that ISPs used, and still do to attract business, was to give away CD-ROMs that install the necessary software and guide you through the process of creating an account. This remains the most popular way to set up an account with an ISP. You can find the CDs not only at computer stores, but also in your local supermarkets, where some charge 50p or so, and newsagents, and some will find their way into your home through your letter box amongst the "junk mail".

Finally, there is always the possibility of visiting an ISP's web site and signing up for an account on-line!

Dial Up Accounts

A Dial Up connection to the Internet uses the same basic technology as the fax machine. You make the connection through an ordinary telephone line, either by swapping your telephone for the cable from the modem inside, or connected to, your computer, or through an inexpensive socket doubler, so that both telephone and computer can remain connected without the need for swapping the plugs, or through an additional telephone socket, installed for the purpose.

To connect to the Internet via a dial-up account means that you take over your telephone line while you are connected. No one else can ring out and incoming callers will find the line busy. By Broadband standards, connection is slow. A typical web page may take six or seven seconds to arrive and be displayed on the computer screen. Some, with a lot of graphics or large photographs on them, could take a minute or more. However, if your main purpose for going on-line is for banking and shopping, then you should find a dial-up account adequate.

Before you decide on a dial-up account, you need to check the REN (Ring Equivalence Number) total of all the equipment connected to your line. Each phone, answering machine or fax will have a REN value marked on it. The total must not exceed four, on any telephone line. Most equipment, these days, has a REN of one, so if you already have a main phone, extension phone and answering machine, you could already be up to three. It is easy to get caught out if you find an existing extension phone with a value of 1.5! If you do exceed your line's REN value, you are likely to find other phones making ringing sounds as you dial a call or as your modem connects to the Internet, and you risk not having any phone ring when an incoming call is made.

Broadband Accounts

For a Broadband connection you need a cable company operating in your area or BT to have implemented ADSL services at your local exchange. Unfortunately, most rural areas are likely to be without Broadband capability for some years to come.

Broadband services are sold on the basis of increased speed compared with a dial-up account, the "always on" nature of the connection, and the fact that you do not lose the use of the phone for ordinary incoming or outgoing voice calls.

Initially, broadband services were offered at a speed of 512kbps. This is about 10 times faster than the maximum speed that a dial-up connection can reach. A dial-up connection has a theoretical maximum of 56kbps, but connections are normally slower than this limit, often only in the mid forties. Broadband works differently and you should always get the "advertised speed" speed of the service for which you contract. With some ISPs, this can be anything between 150kbps and 1,000kbps, with prices scaled appropriately. In essence, at the lower speeds you are sharing the line capacity with others.

This additional speed is mainly of use to those who expect, on an almost daily basis, to receive, that is "download", large volumes of data, typically audiovisual material, such as large high-definition photographs, video, music and so on. For those whose only motivation to connect to the Internet is to do the weekly shopping, then you probably don't need this increased speed and there would be little point in spending the extra money for the service. However, if you can foresee using the Internet more frequently, and your budget will stand it then it is probably worth the extra.

The "always on" aspect has little relevance to the occasional internet shopper. It will save you an initial half a minute while the modem dials the ISPs number and negotiates a connection with the ISPs computer, but has few other advantages. If, on the other hand, you expect a constant stream of urgent e-mails from offspring scattered around the world, then it can be nice to set up your computer to announce the arrival of such messages. E-mails then become much like a written answer phone message. It saves you the business of having, regularly, to go to your computer and check if the expected mail has arrived.

Whether it matters to you that your telephone line is blocked for other use while you are connected to the Internet is another matter and only you can judge its importance.

The Modem

The final component that you need to go on-line is the modem. You need different kinds depending on the type of internet account that you have.

Dial Up Modems

A desktop computer that is running Windows 98 is likely to have a (dial-up) modem already built in. If this is the case then all you will see is a socket in one of the slim metal plates at the back of the computer. This is designed to take a cable similar to that which runs between your ordinary telephone and the wall socket.

Some models include a second socket. Into this you can plug the phone that used to be plugged directly into the wall socket.

If a modem was not supplied with the computer, then is it possible to buy an external modem.   They cost around £15 and are small boxes, often with a variety of small lights on the front that indicate the various signals being sent and received.   A telephone cable runs from the socket at the wall to the modem and another from the modem to the computer. Modems need power.   In older modems this will be supplied through a separate transformer, which must be connected to the mains.   With newer modems, power is supplied through the cable that runs from the computer.

If the prospect of yet another piece of equipment for which you may need to find a power socket worries you, then consider fitting an internal one.   If you don't feel bold enough to tackle it yourself, then a local computer supplier should be able to fit it for you in 15 minutes or so.

Without any casing these are cheaper, around £12, as well as removing a source of clutter on your desk.   You only need to open up the case of the computer and plug it in!   Opening the case is usually just a matter of undoing four or six screws and sliding the casing away to reveals the innards.   An internal modem is supplied as a piece of printed circuit board, approximately 5" by 2".   These printed circuit boards are generally known as "cards".   The card has a number of components soldered to it. On one of the short edges, a narrow metal plate is set at right angles. In this is set the socket, which is seen at the back of the computer once it is installed. On one of the longer sides there are a row of small contacts.

An internal dial-up modem

The contacts on the edge of the card plug into a long socket, referred to as a "slot", that is set at right angles to the back of the computer. There are normally several of these slots on the main circuit board of the computer, and usually a number will already be occupied with other cards, often slightly bigger than the modem. The slot aligns with the hole where the metal plate goes. Initially, the hole is fitted with a blanking plate, held by a single screw that needs to be removed.

If you have a second-hand laptop computer with Windows 98 then it may turn out to have been used originally by peripatetic workers who would return to their office each day. They would swap information with their office computers via floppy disk, rather than the Internet, so modems for these workers were often not fitted at the factory.

However, modems for this type of computer are the easiest to fit retrospectively. Laptops can be expected to be able to use credit card sized devices, known as "PC Cards". These simply push into a slot in the body of the computer. A variety of types of PC Card are available, including those that contain additional data storage, allow connection to a local area network and, of course, those that work as a modem and will cost about £24.

Broadband Modems

If you are opting for a broadband connection then an ordinary modem will not work. You need either an "ADSL modem", if using a conventional telephone line, or a "Cable Modem", if your chosen service provider is a cable company.

If you already have cable television then you already have a cable modem built into your set-top box. If you don't already have a TV contract then a separate cable modem is required, but this will be included in the overall rental package and will be installed by the cable company's own engineer, so purchase is not required.

If you are following the telephone company route, then you will need an ADSL modem. ADSL stands for "Asynchronous Digital Subscriber Line". It's "asynchronous" because the speed at which you send data (upload) is slower than that at which data is sent to you (download). It's "digital" because the ADSL modem does not need to convert the signals between the computer's native digital signals and the analogue squawking noises that are sent down a normal telephone line. Finally it's a "subscriber line", to distinguish it from other services that only operate between telephone exchanges.

An external ADSL modem

When Broadband services first arrived, companies often sold a complete package, which unlike ordinary connections to an ISP, included an initial set-up charge. An engineer would call, do various tests to check on line suitability, install a "microfilter" and provide the ADSL modem. A filter must be connected to any phone socket to which you may also want to have a phone, fax, or answering machine connected. Its function is to separate the broadband traffic on the line from that which works with conventional phone equipment. It is this that enables you to use the phone whilst being on-line.

Now that the market is more mature, the line test and activation for broadband is normally done at the exchange. Buyers can now choose their own modems from a supplier of their choice, the microfilter being included in the package.

If the ADSL modem is not being supplied as part of your account package, you will need to buy your own. They range in price from about £35 to £90. You may see some prices that are higher than that. However, it could be that you are looking at a "Router" rather than a modem. Routers are used where a number of computers are joined together in a network. Networks allow the computers to share resources, such as printers or the data on their disc drives. Increasingly many homes have more than one computer and those families may find it convenient to share their computer resources in this way. In such homes it makes sense to share their broadband connection.

After confirming that the little box you are looking at is a modem you may wonder about the differences in price. This is because the modems can vary in the facilities they offer. Most significantly, they may include a "firewall".

The nature of broadband, which is promoted as an "always on" service, means that subscribers are encouraged to leave their computers on-line for much of the time. When you do this, either because of the flaws in older software, that were mentioned earlier, or because a user is running certain kinds of program that have been badly set up, it is possible for hackers to "attack" a computer. A firewall identifies the unwanted traffic on your line and prevents it from gaining access to your computer. There's more about this in the last chapter.

Internet Connection Costs

As you have to be on-line all the time that you are browsing the web, you may worry how much it will cost. For most people, with a "pay-as-you-go" account on a dial-up connection, it will be about the same as the price of a local phone call, but the special schemes offered by all ISPs may mean it can cost much less. It is difficult to be precise, because the calculation depends on an individual's usage pattern, and prices seem to be falling all the time.

De-regulation of the telephone market has meant that many telephone service providers now have different pricing schemes for ordinary telephone calls and data calls using your computer. Additionally, as competition bites harder, the different companies are constantly changing their pricing policies, introducing new schemes and making occasional special offers. Most ISPs offer up to three connection schemes when using an ordinary line, plus more expensive schemes for those able to have a broadband connection.

Dial-Up

Until the autumn of 2003 the most heavily advertised ISP packages, for use with an ordinary telephone line, offered free calls to the Internet at any time. Instead of paying for telephone calls, you call an 0800 number and are charged a flat monthly fee by the ISP. Typically this is between £10 and £15. These accounts continue to be offered by both the specialist Internet companies, such as BT, Freeserve, AOL and Tiscali and the internet branches of many supermarkets and high-street shops.

For infrequent users of the Internet the "Pay-as-you-go" scheme makes sense. Under such a scheme you pay nothing for your account with your ISP, but instead pay your telephone company through your normal telephone bill, for the time you are on-line. Originally, these calls cost exactly the same as a local telephone call but there has been a trend to charge slightly different rates for voice and data calls. You need to check with your telephone provider what the charge will be.

The third type of account might be called "Limited Hours" and is a combination of the "Anytime" and "Pay-as-you-go" account. It includes a flat-fee element, but limits the time when you may connect without a usage charge. Originally these accounts offered free evening and weekend connection and were aimed at the general family market. However, since the introduction of broadband and the migration of heavy internet users to that service, there is increasing spare capacity at ISPs during the day. So now you are as likely to find one of these schemes offering free daytime weekday connection, as you are one with free evening and weekend use.

Like the "Anytime" accounts you pay your ISP, through a credit card account or by direct debit, and they bill you for both the flat fee and usage charge on a monthly basis. The flat-fee element for these kinds of account is in the order of £5 to £10 per month. In each case the surcharge for out of hours use is about that for a local telephone call.

A daytime limited-hours account is obviously particularly attractive for the retired internet shopper, who can stay on-line for long periods browsing the web without worrying about running up large bills for their use of the telephone. The only concern comes from missing ordinary phone calls, while the line is engaged on internet calls!

Broadband

When introduced, a broadband connection cost in the order of £30 per month, for a 512kbps connection, plus an initial set-up fee that was in excess of £200, but with "do-it-yourself" installation becoming possible, the set-up charges have fallen dramatically. Broadband services are now also offered at a variety of speeds. If you see a dramatic difference in the monthly charge then it is likely this is the reason.

As the market expands rapidly, and when all the players are anxious to grab your business, you are likely to find that the almost constant stream of special deals from the ISPs continues. Typically, these may offer to waive the set-up fee, include the modem, or provide a discount on the first month's subscription.

Summary

It is possible to use almost any computer to access the Internet, including public access computers at local libraries or internet cafés. To connect to the Internet with your own computer you need an account with an Internet Service Provider and the appropriate kind of modem. The type of modem will depend on whether you have a dial-up or the faster broadband connection. For light users, pay-as-you-go dial-up accounts are cost effective. Those expecting to make extensive use of the Internet should opt for an "anytime" account or even broadband.

4

Setting up your ISP Account

Opening an Account with an ISP

There are a number of methods of setting up an account with an ISP. Most people will use a CD-ROM provided by their chosen service provider. If yours is a recent PC then it will usually have Windows XP installed. This has a feature in its New Connection Wizard that avoids the need to obtain a CD-ROM. All you need to do is sit down at your computer and follow the instructions in the wizard. If you have an older version of Windows then you may have icons on your desktop that will connect you directly to an ISP and allow you to set up an account that way. It is also possible to set up the account manually. You might use this method if you have had a hard disc failure or had to re-install Windows, or less drastically, if a friend created the account on a different computer and you now need to copy the appropriate settings to your machine.

The General Process

When you open an account with an ISP you will need to supply your name and address. Most ISPs will also ask you to provide information about how you found out about them.

If you have chosen any account other than a "Pay-as-you-go" type, you will be asked to supply payment method details.

This is true even if you are expecting an initial "free trial" period. Normally, you can choose between debit card, credit card or a direct debit to a bank account. In return, you can expect to be provided with an account number and password that will allow you to access your account information on your ISP's web site. Expect this information to be sent to you via e-mail, which will be sent and ready for you by the time you finish completing the sign-up procedure.

The private area of your ISP's site will show you your current payment method details and allow you to change them. It will also provide you with the invoices and statements issued to you. Note that ISPs do not normally post these to you, a method known as "snail mail" to the internet community, but will e-mail you to tell you that they are now available for you to read, or download, i.e. collect, in this private area of their site.

If you have signed up for a free trial with the ISP, amongst this billing information, echoed back to you when asking you to confirm the details you have entered, or in the e-mail awaiting you, should be the information about how to cancel the account. Obviously you should keep a special note of this, in case you do want to opt out at the end of the period. Take care, too, to read the terms of the free trial. Some have been known to apply to calendar months only, so join on the 25th of the month and you only get five days free trial!

After any billing details, the next most important information you will receive will be the phone number to use (for broadband; your connection settings), a username and password. These last two you will be able to choose yourself, within the limitations set by your chosen ISP. There's more about choosing these in the next section.

Accounts with the various ISPs each work slightly differently. Most ISPs, these days, allow you to use a number of different e-mail addresses through a single account. Some allow you to use an unlimited number of addresses, others only one. Obviously, a small number of addresses can be useful for different family members to use. You might think that having an unlimited number of addresses is pointless. However, if you deliberately use a different address for each company with whom you do business and later junk mail starts arriving, you can easily tell where the company got your address and vow never to use them again!

Apart from a username and password, there are various other technical details that will be required to set up your browser and e-mail software. This may be given to you on screen where you can print it out, but it will always also be sent to you as a file that automatically adjusts these settings for you on your computer. It is always a good idea to print these details if you are given that opportunity. Keep them somewhere safe, in case of problems later.

Selecting a Username and Password

Most people want a username that relates, in some way, to their own name. This is because most ISPs give you an e-mail address that takes the form:

username@ispname

Some, however, particularly those that allow you to have unlimited e-mail addresses, Freeserve is an example, give you an initial e-mail address in the form:

mailname@username.ispname

You pick both the mailname and username parts of this as you create the account. Indeed, at Freeserve, you even have some choice of the ispname part. You can still choose to have an address at "freeserve.co.uk". However, as an alternative you can now opt for "fsbusiness.co.uk", "fsworld.co.uk", "fsmail.co.uk", "fslife.co.uk", "fsnet.co.uk", and perhaps others by now!

Clearly, it is best to consider your names and passwords before beginning the process of opening your account, rather than start thinking about it once you are on-line and filling in the forms on the screen.

If you have a popular name, your preferred option may already be taken. For example, I would expect most ISPs to refuse a new "johnsmith" username by now. Instead the ISP is likely to respond with a number of alternatives. These would be based on the name you select, or perhaps a line from your address. So, if "johnsmith" is already taken, it might come back with a choice of:

johnsmith23	smithjohn
john_smith	smithuk
hill_close11	newport

plus an option to make up a completely different one of your own. If you are happy to pick one of those presented, then do so. If you don't like any of them then you may need to think of something completely different.

That's why its best to think about it before you go on-line. It's too easy to think of something quickly and then think of a much better idea after you have signed up. I never was sure whether the username I saw with 1943 at the end of it meant there were already 1942 people with that name who were already account holders, or if the person concerned was born in that year!

If you are signing up with one of the unlimited-addresses companies, then a username that relates to your forename is probably not the best choice. Instead one that relates to your surname or location might be better. These are some of the ideas that I've seen used:

thesmithfamily	smithnewport
smithofnewport	smithathome
smithhillclose	hillclosenewport
nickname	housename
johnandmary	johnonthenet

The best usernames will be meaningful to your friends and relations, so it is easy to remember and pass on to others and easily pronounceable, so there's no confusion about spelling if you have to give your address over the phone.

Using an ISP's CD-ROM

Now you know what to expect, the sign-up process, using an ISP's CD-ROM shouldn't be difficult. Put it in your drive and it will start automatically. (There will be instructions on the CD-ROM's cover about what to do if your computer is not set to auto-run CD-ROMs.). Once it's started, typically, you'll be presented with a range of options, besides signing up for an account. These might include a video presentation, promoting the benefits of an account; some optional software to use while connected to the Internet, or answers to frequently asked questions, always referred to as "FAQ"s.

The sign-up process itself will be similar to that described later for using the Internet Referral Service. Only the appearance of the screens will be different.

A collection of CD-ROMs obtained from a high-street shop, a computer magazine and through the post

Some of the CD-ROMs you obtain will have special codes on them that need to be entered as part of the sign-up procedure. These have no bearing on the username and password that you choose for your account. They simply help the ISP identify which promotion scheme attracted you to their service.

Using Microsoft's Internet Referral Service

If you don't have a CD-ROM from your provider, then you can turn either to desktop icons, which your computer supplier installed, or to Windows XP's Network Connection Wizard.

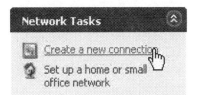

To start this, open the Start Menu, select Connect to, then Show All Connections. This opens the Network Connections window. Towards the top left is the Network Tasks panel. Select the Create a New Connection option in this and, in turn, the New Connection Wizard opens. The first screen of this wizard only explains its purpose and invites you to click the Next button. On the second screen you choose the connection type. Select the first options, Connect to the Internet, and click Next.

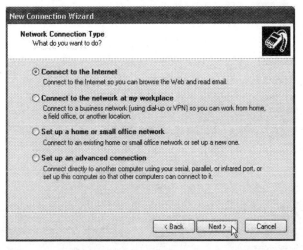

The third screen offers a number of ways to connect including using an ISP's CD-ROM and connecting manually. Once again, the default option is required, "Choose from a list of Internet service providers". After clicking Next, the final screen of the wizard appears. Clicking its Finish button closes the New Connection Wizard and opens an On-Line Services window.

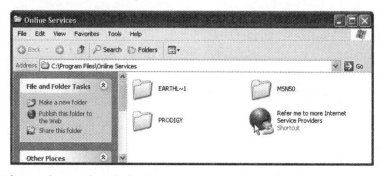

If you have the default Windows installation, and not one customised by your supplier, you'll see a number of folders for US-based ISPs and a "cable and globe" icon. Click on this Refer me to more Internet Services Providers icon. This starts the Internet Connection Wizard. A number of clicks on a Next button are required to get to the point where the computer connects to the Microsoft Internet Referral Service, downloads a list of local ISPs and disconnects again.

Select the icon for the ISP you require, taking care to choose the right account version where there's more than one icon from that ISP, and click the Next button. The next window collects basic information from you.

After completing this screen, the computer will connect to your chosen ISP. You will be taken through a series of screens where you choose what account type you want (assuming you did not make that choice according to the original icon selected) and select your mailname, username, and ispname as required by the ISP you have chosen. These will be checked for acceptability. If a username has already been taken or your proposed password has insufficient characters, you may be asked to enter an alternative. At the end of the process you will be sent a file that you will be instructed to open and not save to disc. This will adjust your browser and e-mail settings, and finally hang up the phone.

Setting up an Account Manually

Most people will not use this option unless a friend or
relation has set up their account for them and the settings are
being transferred to your computer. You might also want to
use it if you have had a catastrophic loss of data, or have had
to re-install Windows. The initial part of this process is
identical to that for using the Internet Referral Service. Only
this time, on the Getting Ready screen, the second option is
chosen.

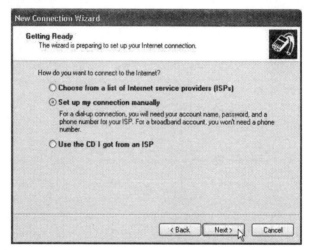

This time the wizard does not finish but takes you to the
Internet Connection screen, where you select whether you are
going to connect using a dial-up modem, using a broadband
connection that requires a user name and password, or using
an always-on broadband connection. The first of these, the
dial-up option, demands the most input by the user, with each
of the other options requiring progressively less.

The first screen in the Dial-Up wizard is headed Connection
Name. It demands a name for the connection. Unless you

have a special reason for an alternative, simply use the name of your ISP. The following screen asks for the Phone Number to Dial. You should have the information required for this entry saved from the time you initially created your account. If you have mislaid it then check to see if there is a Help system on your ISP's CD-ROM and whether it is quoted there. Take care that you do use the correct number. It is easy to enter the ISP's Pay-as-you-go number, and end up wrongly paying for both for the phone calls and the ISP's charge. The next screen requests Internet Account Information.

Again, refer to any note supplied by your ISP before entering your username requested on this screen. With some ISPs it is the part of e-mail address that comes before the "@" symbol (e.g. BTInternet), with others it is the part that comes after the "@" (e.g. Freeserve). In some cases it might be your entire e-mail address (e.g. Tiscali) and it is possible for it to be something else entirely. As always, you are asked to enter the password twice, as it will be cloaked with stars or blobs

as you enter it.   Whether you need to mark the three
checkboxes on this screen will depend on circumstances, but
if you are the sole user of the computer and you have no
other ISP, then the first two boxes would normally be
checked. You should not normally clear the final checkbox,
about the firewall, unless you have alternative software for
the purpose.

The final screen summarises the options that have been
chosen while running the wizard.   Unless you notice any
errors on it, you can click the Finish button.

Note that this option only gets you to the stage where you
can connect to the Internet through your chosen ISP. It has
done nothing to create the appropriate settings within your
browser or e-mail program. Customising Internet Explorer is
covered in Chapter Six. The requirements for e-mail are
explained in the following section. Normally, your ISP will
specify more than is described in this book, but these will be
the minimum required for Internet Banking and Shopping.

E-Mail Settings

In Outlook Express, click "Set up a Mail account" towards the centre of the screen. This opens the first screen of the Internet Connection Wizard that prompts you for your name.

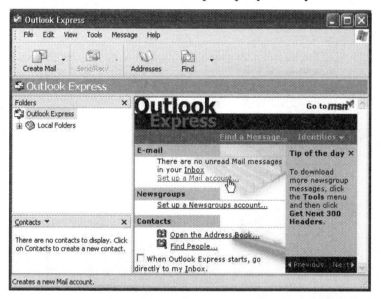

You can also reach the wizard by opening the Tools menu and selecting Accounts. The Internet Accounts dialogue appears (See next page.). Select the Mail tab at the top of this dialogue and then click the Add button at the top right.

A fly-out appears, from which the mail option should be selected. This takes you to the same "Your Name" page of the Internet Connection Wizard.

4   Setting up your ISP Account

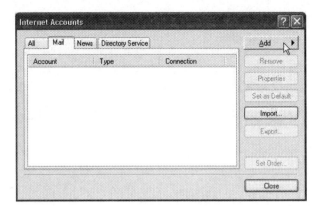

You should enter the name as you would wish it to appear in normal writing, i.e. with initial capital letters.

The following screen prompts you for your e-mail address, and the one after that the E-Mail Server names.

In most cases the incoming mail server will be the default POP3 type, but your ISP will be able to supply all the information you need to enter on this screen. The penultimate, Internet Mail Logon, screen asks for an account name and password.

Normally, these are the same as those you use to connect to the Internet and, as described earlier, may consist of all or part of your e-mail address depending on the ISP. The final "Congratulations" screen merely has a Finish button to click.

Summary

Setting up an Internet account involves little more than supplying a name and address and the username that you wish to use.

Before rushing to open an account, it was suggested that time is taken to think of a number of choices of username in case your first choice has been taken. It always seems possible to think of a better username once you are committed to another.

You can set up an account using an ISP's CD-ROM, Microsoft's Internet Referral Service or you can create the account manually at your chosen ISP's web site. For those setting up the account manually, the process for setting up e-mail was described.

Using the Browser

A Tour round the Browser Window

The Web Browser is the most important tool in the Internet Shopper's basket. It pays to get familiar with its various components and ways to customise it, before going to town to do any real shopping or banking.

As with any Windows program it's topped with a Title Bar. This contains both the title of the document being viewed and the program's name. It will also indicate if the browser is currently off-line. If this shows, it indicates that the user has deliberately selected not to obtain the current version of the page and has loaded a version of the page previously downloaded from the web. The illustration on the next page shows all three of these elements.

The Menu Bar

Under the Title Bar is the Menu Bar, which offers a fairly conventional range of menus. Beneath the Menu Bar are Internet Explorer's three most important controls, the Tool Bar, Address Bar and Links Bar. This area of the window is highly customisable and it is these bars which most people use, to manage virtually all their browsing. If customised appropriately – see the next chapter for some ideas – it is rare to need to use the Menu Bar at all during normal browsing.

The Address Bar

The Address Bar is used to enter a URL manually. If you see a reference to a web site in a magazine or while watching television, then there's no alternative but to make a note of the URL and, when you get to your computer, type it into the browser using this bar. There is no customisation available for the Address Bar, other than whether or not to show the "Go" button. This is the mouse-user's alternative to hitting the Carriage Return, or Enter, key after typing a URL into the bar.

The Tool Bar

While the toolbar is a conventional part of a Windows program, Internet Explorer's is a little unusual as it is frequently customised to show text with some, or all, of the buttons. If you have a small screen, you may find that having the text displayed makes the buttons take up too much space in the window. The range of buttons displayed is customisable, as are their positions on the bar, whether text labels are displayed and their size. Making these changes is described in the next chapter. The default range of buttons include:

Back: This is used to return to the previously viewed page in the current session using Internet Explorer. When it is first launched, this button will always be disabled, since there will be no previously visited page. Note that the button has an associated  drop-down list. Clicking the downwards-pointing arrowhead to the right of the button opens a list of up to 10 previously visited pages. Repeatedly selecting the bottom one on the list allows you to jump quickly back through the pages just viewed. Other ways to revisit pages are discussed in a dedicated section later in this chapter.

Forward: This works in exactly the same way as the Back button. It will be greyed out and inactive until the back button has been used. Then it will enable you to jump forward to return you to a more recently viewed page.

Stop: If for any reason you wish to abandon moving to a page, use the button with the red cross on a page. This button is most useful if a link appears not to be functioning.

Use it when the mouse pointer becomes fixed as an hourglass and the requested page does not appear. Frequently, you find that clicking the original link a second time allows the browser to find an alternative route to the server holding the page and it downloads without trouble at the second try.

Refresh: The button with the circling green arrows forces the browser to fetch the current version of a page. If you are working off-line, reading a cached web page, and realise that information is out of date, then clicking this button forces the browser to go on-line and get the current version.

Home: The house image indicates that this button takes you to your browser's Home Page. The term "Home Page" is used, confusingly, in two different ways on the World Wide Web. The browser's home page is the page that is fetched when the browser is opened. The next Chapter explains how you can set this to any page you wish. A web site can also have a Home Page. This means the "root" page of a web site, designed to be its entry point.

When any of the icons illustrated above is selected, by default the one on the right does not have its "History" label, the button depresses and a panel opens on the left side of the window. Clicking the button a second time closes the panel and raises the button. The contents of the panel vary according to the button clicked.

Search: The Search Panel allows you to enter terms into a "Search Engine". This allows you to retrieve a list of web sites that meet criteria that you select. Its use is explained in Chapter Eight.

Favorites: The spelling of this button will upset many English users, and nothing can be done about it! "Favorites" were first introduced when Microsoft starting bundling Internet Explorer with Windows. They started as web pages that a user could select as important and that they would wish to re-visit at some time. Click on a favourite and it would be loaded into Internet Explorer. Over the years Microsoft has allowed Favorites to spread. Now almost any resource that you encounter while using your computer can be added to your list of Favorites. Click on one and it will be opened in the appropriate program. The use of Favorites to revisit web pages is explained later in the chapter.

Media: This panel duplicates many of the facilities of Windows Media Player. It offers nothing special to those who only want to use the Internet for Banking or Shopping – unless, of course, you are expecting to buy your music on line as downloaded files!

History: This panel provides a list of sites visited over a preset period. The next chapter describes how the user may set the limit, which defaults to 20 days. Items in the History list default to being sorted by date visited. It can also be sorted by site name or frequency of visit, either on the current day or in the overall history. The list always shows the sites as Windows Explorer-like folders, with the individual pages as files within these folders. More details of its use are described in the section, later in the chapter, on revisiting web pages.

The final group of items are frequently part of the customisation made by your ISP, so you may not the see the same set of buttons. This doesn't matter because, as indicated earlier, the buttons are part of the settings that can be changed by the user.

Mail: This button opens your e-mail program, and has a range of options available from the associated drop-down list. Those who only use the web for internet banking or shopping, don't normally need this button and it is one of those that you can consider for removal when customising the tool bar.

Print: This button will print the current web page using the default settings. As many web pages can be very long and need many sheets of paper to print, using this button may not be the best option. The best way to print web pages is discussed in Chapter Seven.

Edit: This button allows you to edit a web page, and by use of the drop-down list select a preferred application with which to do it. Unless you also plan to create a web site of your own, consider removing this button when customising your tool bar.

The Links Bar

Links   Customize Links   Free Hotmail   MSN.com   Radio Station Gu

This bar is the one most likely to be so heavily customised by your ISP that it may look nothing like the default, provided by Microsoft and part of which is illustrated here. Frequently, it is placed on the same line as the Address bar and only its title appears, button-like on the extreme right of the line. When this is the case, a double-headed arrow pointing right will appear immediately to the right of the bar's title. These arrowheads act as a button for a drop-down list, and when clicked, the individual buttons on the bar are shown in a vertical list.

The Links Bar is intended as a collection of immediately accessible links to sites that are of prime importance to you. You should be prepared to customise this heavily. Feel free to delete all the existing buttons and replace them with your choice of links, to match your particular browsing pattern. The method of doing this is explained in the next chapter.

The Status Line

At the bottom of the window is the Status Line. The largest part, to the left, is where messages reflecting aspects of the page being downloaded or currently displayed are shown. When downloading a page, a small part towards the centre will show a progress bar, indicating what proportion of the page has been downloaded so far. In a small box towards the right of the status line, the vital padlock symbol, mentioned in Chapter One, may show. It appears when the page is connected via a "Secure Socket Layer" (SSL). Any information displayed on the page will have been encrypted as it has been sent to you and any text entered on a form on that page will be encrypted as it is sent to the site's owners. The encryption means that anyone trying to intercept this data as it passes through various computers on its way to you will not be able to read or process it. You should only use pages with this symbol displayed to enter critical information, such as credit card account numbers or PINs.

Working with a Browser

Unlike a word processor, which is used to create your own files, or documents, a browser only allows you to view files created by others. This makes it one of the easier programs to use. If you think of a word processor as the equivalent of a video recorder, which so many people find difficult to master, then a browser is no more complicated than the television itself.

While there might be a large number of buttons on your TV's remote control, most people only use a handful of them, the rest being forgotten about in regular daily use. That's not to say that it is not worth knowing what all the controls on your browser do! This section provides the answers.

In Chapter One we saw that a web site is a set of linked files, known as pages, that we request to be sent to us from the computer where they are stored. We call for a page either by entering its address, known technically as its URL (Uniform Resource Locator), into the Browser's Address Bar, or by selecting a link to that file on the page currently displayed in the browser window.

Even if you haven't used the Web itself before, it's almost certain that the principle will be familiar to you. This is because the same technology is used in the Help system built into Windows. Windows' Help files contain pages of information and hyperlinks to move between them. When you search for help on a particular topic you complete the same kinds of "forms" and click similar buttons as you do when providing your name, address and credit card details as you make an on-line purchase or bank transfer. The only difference is that the Help component of a program is normally compiled into a single file, but a web site is held as many separate files. For on-line use this is a benefit as it stops the need to download a complete web site, allowing us to download only the information we request.

Launching Internet Explorer

Having installed the modem and set up your account with your ISP, you'll want to put your Internet skills to the test. Double-click the icon for Internet Explorer that is often installed on your Desktop. Under Windows XP, an option for Internet Explorer will appear at the top of the left-hand column of the Start menu.

Internet
Explorer

You will almost certainly find that as the program opens it will search out and display your ISP's home page. If you are on a dial-up account this means the first thing you will notice is that your computer will attempt to dial your ISP. It will do this because your ISP's web pages will be written to indicate that they have "expired", which the browser will interpret as meaning it has to collect a new copy of the page from your ISP. In this way you are prevented from seeing an old copy. As ISPs get revenue from advertisers, it is understandable that they should wish to force you to see the new advertisements, which may be changed not just every day, but as often as every minute! If you want to stop your computer dialling your ISP, change your browser's home page for one that does not "expire". How to do this is explained in the next chapter.

Moving Round a Web Site

Having opened your first page, whether it's your ISP's or not, you will, undoubtedly, want to move around the site. Frequently, the first page you view on any site is designed to neatly fill the Browser window. The Saga home page shown in Chapter One is an example. This kind of page consists of a wide range of links to other pages and little else. By contrast, Tesco's home page, also illustrated in Chapter One, is much deeper than the space in any browser window will allow. Here we need to know how to move around the page, before considering moving to another page or site.

Moving Round a Page

The original way to move round a page was to use the browser's scroll bar. Those with a wheel-mouse or trackball device have other options. This can include turning on an "auto-scroll" facility.

Whilst pointing at the centre of the browser window tap the wheel or ball. This will place a circular mark on the page, with a dot and two arrowheads in it. The mouse pointer also adopts this dot and two arrowheads shape. Now move the pointer  downwards. As it leaves the circular mark, the upper arrowhead disappears and the page begins to scroll upwards, moving you closer to the bottom of the page being displayed. The further beneath the mark the pointer is moved, and regardless of how far right or left of the circular mark it is moved, the faster the page will scroll. It does this without any further clicking or dragging. Moving the pointer above the circular mark reverses the process and it then scrolls downwards, bringing the top of the page back into view. It is quite feasible to set the page to scroll at reading speed, making auto-scroll a useful technique. A further tap on the wheel or ball, will exit the auto-scroll mode and the mouse will return to its normal behaviour.

For those who find the mouse difficult to use, it is equally possible to use the keyboard. The up and down cursor keys will scroll the page a few lines. The PageUp and PageDown keys scroll a window at a time. Home and End move to the top and bottom of the page. There are many more possible keystrokes. Look up Internet Explorer's Help and search for "Keyboard", then pick the "Shortcuts" item and you will find a comprehensive list of them.

Using Hyperlinks

Virtually every web page will include some hyperlinks, specially marked text, or certain graphics, that can jump you to another page, or a specific point in the current page. You find these links by moving the pointer around the window. Whilst over text, the pointer will appear as an "I-beam", which will be the familiar shape from word processing programs. Over graphics and otherwise empty areas of the page the pointer becomes an arrow. When over a hyperlink the pointer becomes a hand shape with raised index finger. A single click selects the link.

We have FREE software that covers just about every thing you could imagine from desktop publishing, drawing and digital imaging to 3D design and web publishing.

On this page the text links were in blue and underlined, but changed to red as the pointer was moved over them

Typically, text links will be of a different colour from other text on the page, often underlined, though nothing can be guaranteed as each web page author can create links in any way he chooses. Often, items that appear to the newcomer to be text are, in fact, a graphic.

Graphical text is usually fairly obvious, as it will be highly decorated or designed to fit in a specific shape, so enhancing the overall appearance of the page. All that will distinguish a simple graphic from a graphic link will be the shape of the pointer as it passes over the link.

When the pointer hovers over a link, the browser's status line will show the URL of the page to which the link will jump. This can give you some indication of whether the link is internal or external to the current site.

When a link is selected, the browser first checks its cache, a storage area on the hard disc, to see if the page has been visited before. If it has, it will load the page onto the screen from there. If the page is marked as expired (because its author has given the page a time limit), it will connect to the Internet, if not connected already, and request the page from the server on which it is stored.

Once connected to the server, the file is retrieved, along with any graphics or other associated file. This may take a few seconds, up to half a minute of more. On an ordinary dial-up connection, transfer speeds are typically 3-5kb per second. A short all-text page might load in a second or so. However, most pages include some graphics, and these files can be disproportionately large. A typical photograph found on the web might be 100kb or more, and such a file would take 20 seconds to arrive. Much larger files are also possible.

All the files that make up the page are saved on the hard disc as they are displayed on the screen. Exceptions would apply for those files downloaded from a Secure Server, which are not written to the disc. Messages appear on the Status Line as the download takes place, first indicating that it is connecting to the site, then that it is opening the required page. There will usually also be a countdown of the number of graphic files as each is collected, finally finishing with the message "Done", as the final components of the page are displayed. Note that the "Done" message does not reappear, if it is overwritten by an indication of the target of any link that the pointer passes over.

Normally, as the link is clicked, the new page just replaces the one in the current window, but sometimes a link is programmed to open in a new window. It is also possible to force the new page to appear in a new window. Either right-click over the link or select the option "Open in New Window" from the menu that appears or hold the SHIFT key down as you click on the link.

Some web pages spawn new pages in additional windows without the user selecting a link. These new windows may have no menu or toolbars and are known as "Pop-ups". They frequently contain adverts from companies that pay the main site to display their pages in this way. Whilst some companies manage to find sympathetic sponsors for their site, many appear to accept anyone's money. As a result, Pop-ups are usually regarded as nothing more than intrusive junk and are widely condemned.

It is also possible to use the keyboard to move between hyperlinks. Repeatedly tapping the Tab key will cycle through all links on a page, plus any form controls, explained in the next section. After finding the final link, the focus jumps to the Address bar before returning to the first link on the page. Having found the required link, hitting the Carriage Return or Enter key will select the link. If you skip past a link by mistake, hold the Shift key while hitting the Tab key. This will reverse the order of movement through the links, so you can return to the one you overshot. To open a link in a new window, keyboard users can echo one of the methods used by mouse users and hold the Shift key as they hit the Enter, or Carriage Return key.

Revisiting Web Pages

Forcing you to download the latest version of a page every time you attempt to re-visit is programmed into a great number of sites, especially those that rely on advertising income, or where its aim is to sell you the latest "bargain". As already mentioned, your ISP's site is likely to be one of these. Non-commercial sites are much less likely to force you on-line and it is possible to revisit such pages without having to go on-line.

Internet Explorer provides a number of different ways of reaching a page that's been visited before. The techniques you choose will depend on your use of the web and the types of sites that you visit. Before explaining the options you need to understand some special cases when a browser cannot fetch a file from the local store (your hard disc).

- When page authors insert code to tell the browser that they must fetch the current version of the page from the server or that a page "expires" after a certain date or time.

- When you view pages on a secure server, such as those where you give your credit card details. These are not stored on your hard disc.

In either of these cases, the browser will attempt to dial your ISP, in order to get the current version of the page. You will find the "Connect to" dialogue appearing and you must go on-line to revisit the page. In other cases, when the "Connect to" dialogue appears, you can click on the "Work Offline" button and the pages will appear, loaded from your hard disc.

Some ISPs do not use the standard dialler software. The only reason for supplying non-standard software often appears to be nothing more than to force you to go on-line or stay on-line longer than necessary. All that does is increase your phone bill unnecessarily and so make one of the company's subscription schemes, frequently in the order of £15 per month,

Dial-up Connection

Select the service you want to connect to, and then enter your user name and password.

Connect to: Freeserve

User name: bankingandshopping.freeserve

Password: ●●●●●●●●●●●●●●●●

☑ Save password

☐ Connect automatically

[Connect]   [Settings...]   [Work Offline]

appear better value, as you then get "free" internet phone calls. However, if you only go on-line occasionally and make sure that internet activity is limited to evening and weekends, then it may be better to stick to a pay-as-you-go account and pay for those phone calls. Of course, while shopping or doing your banking you do need to be on-line, or you won't be able to place orders or make transfers. However, when surfing for other reasons, pay-as-you-go customers can save money by using the techniques outlined here and those with other accounts may well find the techniques useful for speeding up their surfing..

Back and Forward Buttons

The Back and Forward buttons allow you to move to view the pages visited during the current session of Internet Explorer. By default these buttons appear at the left end of the Toolbar. Initially they are both inactive and greyed out. After moving forward to a new page the back button becomes active (as shown here). If you then click the Back button you return to the previous page and the Forward button becomes active. You can, of course, then click on the Forward button to get back to the page you just left.

Each of these buttons has an associated drop-down list. Click on these and you see a list of up to nine of most recent past (or next forward) pages. Click on an item in the list and you can jump directly to one of these pages. If you have visited

many pages in the session, and want to move to one of the first pages you visited then the quickest way is to opt for the History item that appears at the bottom of the list once the list has grown to two entries.

Note that long page names will not be fully displayed and get cut off, and that not all web page authors are very good at providing proper page titles to appear on the list. So don't be surprised if the page names on the list appear to be in an author's code or, inconveniently, show only the site title, rather than the individual page title.

You also need to be aware that some page authors force pages to start in new windows. You can sometimes find that the Back and Forward buttons appear to go greyed out during a browsing session. In that case you will find that you now have an additional Internet Explorer button on the task bar, assuming that you do not have so many windows open that they have begun to group themselves as a list under a single button. Where a page does appear in a new window, the original instance of Internet Explorer will have retained its own history and the Back and Forward buttons on that window will allow you to complete any navigation to the page desired. Overall, it may be quicker to use the history option.

History

While the Back and Forward buttons allow revisiting of pages in a single Internet Explorer window, the History facility saves all the pages that you have visited (up to a 20 day limit, unless you have altered the default. See the Browser Customisation section for details). To access the History list, click the History button (the Clock with anti-clockwise arrow) on the toolbar. You can also use the keyboard shortcut Ctrl+H, or the View menu (Select Explorer Bar, then History). This opens up a panel, known as an Explorer Bar, on the left side of the browser window.

The default view of the History Explorer Bar shows the previously visited pages in date order. A calendar "grid" icon appears beside the periods covered, which initially are for a weekly period and then daily for the current week. Click on any of the calendar icons and a set of yellow folder

icons appear, one for each site visited in that period. Click on a site icon and a list of pages visited at that site appears.

The lists of sites and pages can be very confusing, as many commercial sites are constructed as a maze of related sub-sites, so you may not immediately recognise the site and page names that are listed. Additionally, as noted for the Back and Forward button lists, web page authors are frequently very poor at giving their pages meaningful names.

Apart from the date-ordered history list, you can click the "View" button at the top of the list and select alternative views of the history list. The Search facility in the History list is, of course, limited to pages stored in your history.

The History panel can be closed either by clicking the "X" button at the top right of the panel or clicking the, now depressed, History button on the toolbar.

Favorites

Pages that you know you will want to re-visit can be stored as "Favorites" (Note the American spelling!). Some web pages may refer to "Book marking" the page, or adding it to your "Hot List". The authors of these pages are used to using browsers other than Internet Explorer, which use these terms to refer to their version of the "Favorites" function.

Favorites	Tools	Help

Add to Favorites...

Organize Favorites...

📁 East Walton Info ▸
📁 Finance ▸
📁 ISPs and Hosting ▸
📁 Links ▸
📁 Maps ▸
📁 OldLinks ▸
📁 Other ▸
📁 Own sites ▸
📁 Shopping ▸
📁 Software Sources ▸
📁 Technical Info ▸
📁 Waterways ▸
📁 WEB Guides ▸
📁 BBC - Radio
📁 BT Directory Enquires
📁 East Winch Cottage
📁 Google Advanced Search

To add a page to your Favorites, simply open the Favorites menu and click on "Add to Favorites". This opens the "Add Favorite" dialogue. Take the opportunity to give the page a brief meaningful name if the author's is not helpful.

By default, newly added pages are simply added to the menu. However, the dialogue has a "Create in" button that reveals additional facilities that enables you to organise favourites into folders as you go along enabling the results shown on the Favorites menu here. Note that the "New Folder" button will create the new folder as a sub-folder of currently selected one.

Add Favorite [?][X]

☆ Internet Explorer will add this page to your Favorites list.   [OK]

☐ Make available offline   [Customize...]   [Cancel]

Name: [Argos - Buy OnLine]   [Create in <<]

Create in:
📁 ISPs and Hosting
📁 Links
📁 Maps
📁 OldLinks
📁 Other
📁 Own sites
📁 Shopping
📁 Software Sources
📁 Technical Info
📁 Waterways

[New Folder...]

The Add Favorite Dialogue, extended by using "Create in"

Although most pages will be stored locally, they will still be subject to your history limits, and will, if not viewed again, be deleted from your system. The function of the "Make available off-line" feature is to over-ride the History settings and keep the files always available. Once the option is set, the Customize option becomes available. This takes you through a wizard that allows you to set a schedule for checking the page and downloading the latest version automatically.

This dialogue allows you to organise your Favorites

Once you have more than a handful of folders in your favourites and you continue to add more pages to them, it will become necessary to organise them further. At its simplest level this can just mean dragging individual page icons into some sort of order. It is also possible to drag folder icons around the menu. Alternatively, you can use the "Organize Favorites" dialogue. You can also use this dialogue to create new folders and select one or more files and/or folders and then move, rename or delete them.

As well as working through the menu system, it is also possible to use the toolbar button to open the Favorites Explorer Bar, which will replace the History or Search Explorer Bars, if they are displayed. The facilities available are exactly the same as those available from the Favorites menu. The "Add" and "Organize" buttons access the same dialogues as those reached from the Favorites menu.

Links

The Links Bar contains a number of buttons that will take you directly to a limited range of web sites. There is nothing fixed about the set of links on the Links Bar and when customised the Links Bar is ideal for those who regularly re-visit a limited range of web sites. Right-click over any of the buttons and you open a menu that allows you to delete or rename buttons created by your ISP.

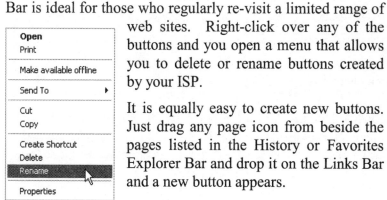

It is equally easy to create new buttons. Just drag any page icon from beside the pages listed in the History or Favorites Explorer Bar and drop it on the Links Bar and a new button appears.

If you add too many buttons to appear within the width of the browser window then, as shown in the section offering a tour of the browser window, a small double arrow button will appear enabling you to reach the additional buttons. However, once it grows to this extent, the bar offers little advantage over ordinary "Favorites".

Interacting with a Web Site

When banking or shopping on the Internet, there'll come a point when you'll need to provide the web site's owner with some information, your name, address, credit card numbers, PINs, and so forth. You'll also want to tell the owner what it is you want to buy, product, size, colour, quantity and so on, or how much you want to transfer between bank accounts. This is usually done through a "form". Forms can include a variety of components. These will all be familiar to users of Windows dialogue boxes.

Select your Toshiba product line ▼
Select your Toshiba product line
DynaBook
Dynapad
Equium
GS Series
Infinia
Libretto
M Series
Magnia
PageLaser
Portege
Satellite
Satellite Pro
T-Series Laptops
TE-Series
Tecra
Toshiba Value Priced Systems

Drop-down lists allow you to pick from a predetermined set of options. Click the downward pointing arrowhead to the right of the line, and a set of options to pick from appears. Click the required option and the list closes up, with the newly selected option now showing in the original line. Long lists will include scroll bars.

Check Boxes permit a mix of non-conflicting options to be selected. Select the option by clicking the box, when a tick will appear. A second click de-selects the option. There may be only a single box or many.

☑ My billing and shipping address are the same.

Radio Buttons allow you to pick one option, from a set of mutually exclusive ones. Click an option and the associated circle is filled. Click another option to change the selection.

Payment Method:* ⦿ Credit/Debit Card
                  ○ Wire Transfer or other Alternative Payment Method.

Text Boxes are for entering free text, perhaps for a name or phone number. There may be a limit to the number of characters that you can type into the box, and that limit could be more than is visible within the box area. In that case the text will scroll within the box.

To: [   ] in [United Kingdom   ▼]
Enter mobile phone number, e.g. 07123456789 (please don't enter any spaces or a country code)

Message: [   ] Characters remaining:
                                                    [130]

**A form for sending a text message to a mobile phone.
It includes a Text Box, Drop-down List and Text Area and an
automated control showing the characters remaining**

Text Areas are multi-line text boxes, perhaps for the message to be printed on the card to be sent with a floral bouquet. They may include a scrollbar facility, in case you type more than the box itself will accommodate, or as with single-line text boxes there may be a limit to the number of characters that may be entered.

Buttons will be used to process the form in some way. Those illustrated here will send the form's contents to the site owner, or clear the form, to allow the re-entry of the data.

Summary

An introduction to the browser interface was followed by a description of what to expect when launching Internet Explorer and how to use it to navigate round web sites.

Some techniques for re-visiting web pages without being forced to go on-line were explained and how to interact with pages which require information to be entered.

Customising the Browser

Making Changes

The way Internet Explorer is set up when you start to use it is determined both by Microsoft and, almost certainly, your Internet Service Provider. Internet Explorer obtains some of its defaults from the way you have set up Windows. ISPs will also customise Internet Explorer in ways that encourage you to use their web site more.

There's nothing to stop you making changes too. Indeed, it is to be encouraged, so that the browser suits the way that you work, the size of your screen, its resolution, the sites you visit and so that it compensates for any difficulties that you may have with your vision.

Setting the Home Page

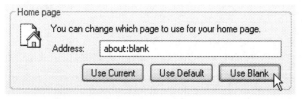

Almost certainly, your ISP will have set your browser to visit your ISP's web site whenever you launch it. You can change this behaviour on the "General" tab of the "Internet Options" dialogue, which is found on the "Tools" menu.

The "Internet Options" dialogue with its default settings

Unless your ISP has set up your system with further modifications, "Use Blank" should stop your computer trying to connect to the Internet every time it is started. It will show "about:blank" in the text area.

"Use Current" sets the page currently displayed to be the one that opens when you start Internet Explorer. One possible approach is to set this to your preferred Search Engine. "Use Default" will force Internet Explorer to open the page set when you created your account with your ISP or when it was installed if you haven't yet set up an account.

Setting the History Period

By default, Internet Explorer stores all the pages viewed for 20 days. This is known as the History. (Certain pages, such as those viewed over a "secure connection", will not be retained.)

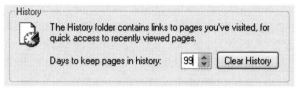

You can keep pages for longer than this by adjusting the number of days set in the History section under the "General" tab of the "Internet Options" dialogue. (Type the number into the spin-wheel box, rather than using the up and down buttons, or it will take forever to adjust!)

Setting Accessibility Options

Most web site authors, especially of commercial sites, seem to assume that users have perfect eyesight. They frequently design their sites to squeeze in the maximum number of adverts and links in an effort to keep the user's interest. As a result they set the text small and sometimes use a font that is difficult to read. The colour schemes they choose may also not be the best for older eyes. The Accessibility options will help overcome this problem, though it must be admitted, usually at the cost of the lovingly created design that the author intended.

At the bottom of the "General" tab of the "Internet options" dialogue is an "Accessibility" button. Click this and the "Accessibility" dialogue opens. The top, "Formatting", group of options will remove the settings defined by the web page's author. Try selecting any or all of the options and see if you find the result easier to read. Checking the boxes will replace the author's settings with the settings defined in your browser. You can change these if you don't like the results you now have.

The User style sheet setting is beyond the scope of this book and requires some knowledge of "Cascading Style Sheets" and web page creation. If you have pronounced difficulties with your vision it would be worthwhile consulting someone with these skills and get them to create a personalised style sheet, which can comprehensively override all the settings defined by the author of any web page. Your local Social Services Department should have such contacts.

The Accessibility Dialogue, reached through the button on the General tab of the Internet Options dialogue

To the left of the Accessibility button on the Internet Options dialogue, are buttons that open the dialogues that allow you to set your preferred fonts and colours. The settings made here are applied to any page where the author has not defined a preference.

The Colors dialogue defaults to show "Windows colors", that is the colours defined under the Appearance tab of the Display Properties dialogue within the Windows Control Panel. Clear this check box and you have the freedom to show whatever colours you like for the text and background colours. The Hover color option, when checked, defines the colour that any hyperlinks show when the mouse moves over a link. Experiment with the options you find here to get the results that you want.

The default web page font is "Times New Roman", a font that works well in printed documents, but can appear rather jagged on a computer screen. You might prefer "Arial" or the font "Tahoma", which was specifically designed for on-screen use.

The plain text font is used where the page author has defined a mono-spaced font. The default is "Courier New". Mono-spaced fonts are reminiscent of old typewriter fonts as every letter from "i" and "l" to "M" and "W" is the same width.

Maximising Screen Space

One way to ensure that you get the largest amount of space on your screen to display web pages is to hit the F11 key. This not only maximises the window but also removes many of the standard components of a window from view. Some adjustments to this view of the window are possible by right-clicking over the toolbar that is left on the screen. Hitting F11 for a second time returns the screen to normal.

If such a drastic approach does not appeal to you then you can create more space in the main part of the browser window by removing or re-positioning the various tool bars at the top of your screen.

First make sure that the toolbars are not locked. If there are no vertical lines of dots at the left-hand end of the various bars, then the bars are locked. To unlock them, right-click anywhere over the main toolbar, except over the Back or Forward buttons and you should be able to find a menu with a "Lock the Toolbars" option displayed with a tick. Click that option to unlock the bars.

Move and Remove Tool Bars

Now you will be able to access the various pointers you need. As ever, they vary depending on the component that you point at:

Resize: (Seen when dragging the division between tool bars and main window) Drag up and down to compress or expand the area allotted to the toolbars.

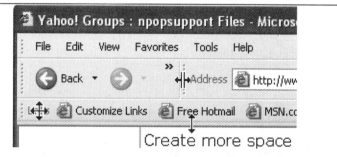

Some trickery allows you to see the various pointers that appear when dragging in the toolbar area

Move: (Seen when dragging a toolbar name) Drag and drop any of the visible bars elsewhere in the toolbar area.

Adjust: (Seen when dragging the dotted bar at the left end of any toolbar) Drag and drop any of the visible bars elsewhere in the tool bar area.

You can remove any toolbar completely by right-clicking anywhere over an empty part of the toolbar area and selecting its name on the pop-up menu. The currently displayed items are shown with a tick. Clicking an unticked item adds it back again.

Earlier it was mentioned that you could use the Links tool bar as a set of "Super Favorites". If you have few Favorites, then you may feel the Links Bar is redundant and be inclined to remove it. However, you could choose to use it as a scratch pad for links to sites of temporary interest, rather than give them permanent "favourite" status. It is, for instance, quicker to add a site to the Links Bar than it is to add it as a favourite. Instead of clicking a link, drag it to the Links Bar and drop it there. Or if you realise a recently visited page may be worthy of further interest, open the History panel and drag its icon to the Links Bar. To remove a Link for which you have no further interest, just right-click it and choose delete from the pop-up menu.

Customize the Toolbar

The Customize Toolbar dialogue may be opened by right-clicking in the Standard Toolbar area and choosing the "Customize..." option. Note that the option will not appear when right-clicking on other parts of the toolbar area. The dialogue has three functions. Perhaps most importantly, it allows you to choose which icons to show on the toolbar. It also controls whether to show, hide or show only some of the text associated with the standard toolbar icons and allows you to choose whether the toolbar should show large or small icons.

If you have not yet opened the Customize Toolbars dialogue, it is also possible to hide the text labels by dragging upwards on the division with the main window, as described in the section above.

You do not lose the button descriptions if you decide not to show the button text, as a tool-tip will appear when the pointer hovers over the button. Hiding the button text can create a lot of extra room on the toolbar without losing access to the information about what any icon does and, depending on screen size, two bars can often be accommodated on one line.

The Customize Toolbar dialogue Box, set to show small icons and to remove the default text labels to the toolbar buttons. Additional buttons have been added to the toolbar too!

Apart from deleting toolbar buttons that you may not require, obvious candidates for selection include "Font Size" and "Print Preview". Font Size, which can also be controlled from an option on the View menu, gives you the ability to adjust the size of the text both on screen and on any printed copy of the page. Note that on many sites, you need to have set the Accessibility option, discussed earlier, for this to have any effect. Print Preview allows you to check, before printing, how many sheets of paper printing will consume and on what page number a vital part of the information will appear, allowing you to print just that one. The best options for you to choose to select or remove will depend on the size of your screen and how you normally use Internet Explorer.

Summary

Internet Explorer is invariably customised by your ISP, sometimes in ways that are not best for your way of working.

Changes to the default settings were explained which could be particularly helpful to those with pay-as-you-go Internet connections and those with poor vision.

Customising the toolbar both to maximise screen space and to provide for easier ways of working were also explored.

Keeping Records

If Something Goes Wrong

We've all heard the shop assistant's warning, "Keep the receipt, in case you need a refund!" Similarly, it is prudent to keep records of your purchases as you order them when making a purchase on-line. If things do go wrong, you can then turn to them, both to remind yourself of what you did and what happened when, and also, in the last resort, to provide evidence in any claim we need to make.

There are a couple of ways that we can do that. Either we need to save the information as a computer file, or it needs to be on paper. In this chapter we'll look at the best way to do both these tasks.

Printing Web Pages

The simplest way to print a web page is to click on the Print toolbar button. However, clicking on this button is rarely the best way to print a page.

Most printed documents start with a title or heading. Look at the typical web page and you are likely to find a large collection of navigation links across the top of the page. You may also find a menu running down the left-hand side and perhaps a string of advertisements to the right. Somewhere in the middle of the page, surrounded by all this stuff, you find the material in which you are really interested.

It is rare for the navigation links, menus and adverts to be something that you would want to commit to paper. Certainly, most of these will only be of use when you are looking at the page on the computer screen. If that is the case, why print them?

Another issue will often be the amount of paper it takes to print a page. A single web page might take many sheets of paper to print in its entirety. If you only want part of that information printed, then you need to find out where, in amongst all those pages, it will print.

Print Preview

With some of these factors in mind, before printing complete web pages, it is a good idea to select Print Preview on the File menu. You may also want to read Chapter Five, which explained how to add a Print Preview button to the toolbar.

When you select Print Preview a new window appears that overlays the main Internet Explorer window. It has no menu bar and a new toolbar of its own. This toolbar has a fixed range of buttons. The first takes you to the Print Dialogue, the second to the Page Setup Dialogue, both discussed later in the chapter.

Then comes a set of buttons that allow you to move through the pages, as they will appear in print. The outer double-arrows take you to the first and last page that will be printed. The inner single-arrows take you to the previous and next pages. In the centre is a text box, into which you can type a page number. Hit the carriage return key to jump to that page. Also here, is an indication of the total number of sheets needed to print the web page. Note that the scroll bar in this window is unusual. Normally, the size of the block on the bar indicates the proportion of the entire document that is visible in the window. This one is different as it indicates only the proportion of the currently displayed page.

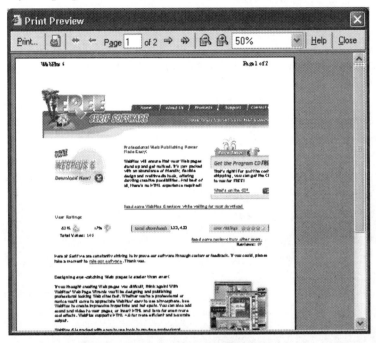

The Browser in Print Preview mode

The following set of controls control the zoom. The magnifying glass and page icons, with plus and minus signs on them, magnify and reduce the image of the currently displayed page. Alternatively, you can use the drop-down list to select a given size. Even if you cannot read the fine text of a page in this view, you do get an idea of the general page layout.

If you are previewing a page that is laid out in frames an additional control appears on the toolbar.   Frames are discussed in the section on the Options Tab of the Print Dialogue.

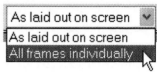

Finally, there are buttons to open Help and close the preview window.

Using the print preview feature can help you make decisions on any adjustments to control the amount of paper used. Depending on how the author designed the page, you may be able to adjust the size of the text, reducing it enough to stop the printout flowing just onto the top of the final page. You will certainly be able to adjust the margins, to squeeze a little more text on each page, or force an image onto a different page. The Print Preview will also remind you of the header and footer settings, which you might choose to adjust.

If you check the Print Dialogue, covered in a later section, you will see that it is possible to select part of a web page for printing. Unfortunately, there is no way to preview how such a selected portion of the page will look when printed. Print Preview will always show complete pages.

The Page Setup Dialogue

If you use the print preview facility and decide that the Page Setup needs adjusting you can open the dialogue directly from the toolbar. You can also call up the dialogue from the File menu of the main window.

Most of the settings on the dialogue are straightforward. Only the Headers and Footers section needs any explanation. Each of the lines may include a number of codes as well as the text that you wish to appear here. Some of the codes act as "system variables" and on both the preview and printout the codes are substituted for the text that the variables represent. The remaining codes control the alignment of the text. You will also see that the default header includes plain text as well as both system variable and alignment codes.

**The Page Setup Dialogue
showing the default header and footer codes**

Header and Footer Codes

&w   The Window Title

&u   The Page Address (URL)

&d   Date in short format

&D	Date in long format
&t	Time in regional format
&T	Time in 24hr format
&p	Current page number
&P	Total number of pages
&b	Immediately following text is right-aligned
&b&b	Text after first "b" is centred and second "b" is right-aligned.

If you need a reminder of the codes, an on-screen version can be obtained by clicking the "?" at the top of the dialogue. This adds a "?" to your pointer, after which you can click the "Header and Footers" area of the dialogue to open it.

The Print Dialogue

Depending on your system, the Print dialogue may have a number of tabs but only the General and Options tabs always appear. When the dialogue opens the General tab will be displayed. This has three distinct sections where you can select the printer, the range of pages to be printed and the number of copies to be printed.

In the Select Printer section the default printer, indicated with a tick against its icon, will be selected. Click on a different printer to select an alternative. The "Preferences" button will take you to a dialogue with options that apply to the selected printer. For example some printers allow you to turn off colour printing, or print in "economy mode" to save ink or use double-sided printing to save paper. The "Find Printer" button is normally only used when your computer is connected to a network.

The "Print to file" option, is somewhat specialised. It is a facility that enables you to take "an image" of the printout, on disk, to another computer. That computer must have the same make and model of printer as you, but it needn't have the same programs installed.

The "Page Range" section controls what is printed and might be better termed "Sheet Range" as it controls the number of sheets of paper that will be used. By default, the "All" option will be selected and the entire contents of the web page will be printed. As web pages can be large, it might take many sheets of paper to print a web page completely.

The "Pages" option can be set so that only the page number, or page range, specified is printed. The trouble with this option is that it is almost impossible to guess how many sheets of paper it will take to print a page, and where, in this range, the information that you want will appear. In order to take advantage of this option, you need to have selected Print Preview before opening the Print dialogue. Using Print Preview, you can scan through a web page, as it will appear in print, before deciding what page range to print.

The "Selection" option is greyed out unless something on the page has been selected. To select a portion of the page simply drag the pointer over the part of the page in which you are interested. Depending on the design of the page, it may not be possible to select exactly what you want, but items like menus and navigation links can often be excluded from a selected area.

The "Current Page" option is greyed out unless you access the Print dialogue from the Print Preview. In this case the "current" page is the one visible in the Print Preview window.

Printing Frames

To understand the options available on the Options tab you need to be aware of whether the page you intend to print is set in "frames". Most web pages that you see will be a single document, illustrated with a number of separate picture files, some of which may include animations. All of these elements must be downloaded for the page to be completed.

It is also possible for a web page author to arrange things so that a number of separate documents are displayed at the same time. The page is then said to be in frames, since each of the documents will be displayed in its own frame.

The main advantage of arranging things in this way is that certain elements of the "page" can be made to remain in view, whilst others change. Most commonly the technique will be used to keep the site's main menu or navigation system always in view, but it can be used for any number of other reasons, as the designer chooses.

This screen is divided into four unequally sized frames

It is immediately obvious if a page is "framed" if there are bars dividing parts of the window or if there is a scroll bar somewhere in the middle of the window, or if the scroll bar at the right side of the page does not reach all the way down the side of the page or is split into more than one bar.

If there are frame bars these can normally be dragged to resize the individual frames, enabling different proportions of the individual document files to be displayed. However, it is also possible for the page's author to disallow this.

Of course, scroll bars will not appear unless material within that frame overflows the space allocated to it, so the scroll bars will not become visible until the window is deliberately re-sized smaller. Even then scroll bars may not appear, as it is possible for an author to prevent text from being allowed to scroll.

The Tesco Home page, illustrated on the previous page, is typical of a framed page. This one is divided into four. The top left frame holds only the Tesco logo and, directly under it, the word "Home". Beneath that, bounded by the scroll bar on its right, is a menu frame. To the right of that, and a little taller, is the main document frame. Finally, above this is another two-part menu, the lower part of which appears as a set of tabs, with the left-most one selected. With an understanding of frames, you can interpret the options shown on the second tab of the Print dialogue.

The Options Tab

If the current page in the browser is not in frames, the main option here will be greyed out. However, if it is framed then, by default, the first option, "As laid out on screen", will be selected and the preview to its left will show an illustrative page consisting of three frames displayed in a browser with those three frames as they will appear when printed. Note that the preview always shows three frames in this arrangement, regardless of the actual layout of the page.

The second option is only active if one of the frames has been selected. If selected, the preview shows a subtly different layout for the preview. There is still a single sheet of paper illustrated, but it shows a single colour, reflecting

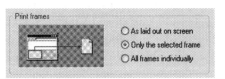

the colour of the frame that is selected in the preview.

The Print Dialogue with its Options tab selected

The final option shows how all the frames will be printed but each on its own sheet of paper. Obviously, in all cases, it is possible for a frame to take more than one sheet of paper to

print the contents of the frame, but there is no doubt that the final option will use more paper that the other two.

The other two options on the page will also add significantly to the number of sheets of paper that will be used and should be used with some caution. Imagine the consequences of using "Print all linked pages" on a page with extensive menus, such as the Tesco page illustrated here, where each of the menu options links to another page, each of which might take several sheets of paper to print completely.

The "Print table of links" is a little more sparing with paper. It simply produces a list of the pages linked to the current one, showing the text that forms the link and the URL of the link. This can be useful, if you think you may want to visit these links in the future, but not for some time after your history will have expired. (Using the Browser's History feature was described in the section on Revisiting Web Pages, in Chapter Five.)

Printing Background Colours

Sometimes when you print a web page, large areas of colour will be missing. This is usually because these are "backgrounds". Commonly, if printed, these backgrounds do little more than consume ink. In this case you will want to retain the default setting, which is not to print them. However, if you need them, perhaps because very light coloured text is invisible without the dark background seen on screen, then you need to adjust this.

To turn them on go to the "Advanced" tab of the "Internet Options" dialogue and click on the box labelled "Print background colors and images".

Screen Dumps

There can be occasions where it might seem a waste of paper to print a web page. Certainly, if the sole reason for printing the page is as a precaution in case the e-mail confirming the purchase order does not arrive, then you might consider it a waste of paper – until the occasion when you need the document! One way to deal with this is to take a "screen dump". A screen dump is a digital image of the screen. A number of screen dumps can be pasted into a WORD document and the document saved at the end of the purchase procedure. Once the e-mail arrives, the document can then be deleted.

To take a screen dump simply tap the "Print Screen" key, normally found at the top of the keyboard to the right of the "F12" function key. If your screen is large enough and you don't normally operate with the browser window maximised, then you may only want a "window dump" rather than a dump of the whole screen. To limit the image to the active window, hold the ALT key when tapping the Print Screen key. Contrary to what you might expect, given the name of the key, the image is not printed but instead placed on the clipboard, in the same way that in WORD, "cut" or "copy" will place selected text on the clipboard.

Next swap to WORD and paste the dump into the empty document you have ready for the purpose. As your hands are already over the keyboard, the quickest way to do this will not be with the mouse. Continue to hold down the ALT key and hit the TAB key until the icon for the WORD document becomes selected in the task-switching window that appears. Hold CTRL and hit the letter "V" to paste the dump into WORD, then hold ALT once more and tap TAB to return to Internet Explorer.

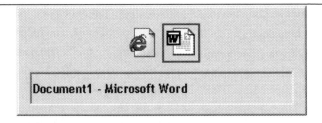

**The Task Switcher Dialogue, seen when using "ALT-TAB",
with a WORD document selected**

Note that this is only a method for taking an image of the visible contents of the window, so if the window has scrolled it may be necessary to take a number of dumps for each window in order to capture the complete contents of the page.

Saving Web Pages

Another way to keep a record of a web page that you are currently viewing is to save it. You can do this by selecting "Save as..." from the File menu. When the dialogue opens, drop down the "Save as type:" list and select the "Web archive (*.mht)" option. (The exact name of this option varies slightly depending on the version of Internet Explorer that you are running.) This is preferable to the option to save the "Web Page, complete" as that option separates the graphics on the page into a dedicated folder, which makes it slightly more difficult to manage if ever the web page file is moved from its original location.

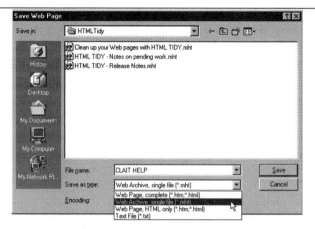

**The correct option is to save a web page
and all its graphics into a single file**

Although this may seem a better option than taking a screen dump, some pages on secure sites will not save properly to disc. If this is going to happen, however, a warning dialogue should appear. If this happens then you will need to use one of the techniques described earlier to make your record of the transaction.

Summary

It is important to keep records of your transactions in case you need them should problems develop with your order. Any order is normally confirmed by e-mail, but if this does not arrive then copies of the pages visited, showing the details that you entered, may be the only evidence you have of the order.

7 Keeping Records

This chapter described how to print web pages, save copies of your screen during the purchase process and save web pages to disc.

Finding What You Want

How to Find What You Want

Everyone has the same problem! The Web is so big, and growing all the time. How do you find what you are looking for? Experienced surfers will probably reply that you should, "Use a Search Engine". The trouble with that is that it's a bit like trying to find how to spell a word, when all you have is a dictionary. You know the word is in there somewhere, but if you don't know how to spell it, how are you going to find it?

There are a number of approaches, and which is best will depend on what you are seeking. You may know that you need a particular shop. You may know the product you want, but want to know where to find it cheapest, or who can send it to you fastest. You may not know what you want and are "just looking" for an inspired present for a birthday or other special occasion.

This chapter explains the components of a web page address, which should help your understanding of what is worth trying to type into the Address Bar, explains the search tool facilities built into Internet Explorer, and provides some history on web searching tools, which forms a good introduction to the following two chapters.

Entering an Address

Perhaps the easiest kind of site to find is one for a nationwide chain of shops. Just enter its URL in the address bar then hit the carriage return key or click the GO button. If you don't know the URL, then you could have a go at guessing it. This approach is often overlooked, but if all you are interested in is large nationally known organisations, then you may strike lucky. As you can see from those listed in Appendix One, most URLs follow a pattern and it is likely to be based on the company name.

Components of a URL

It is worth understanding a little of how a URL is put together, as it can allow you to make better guesses at what a company's web address might be. Normally a company's URL would take this form:

http://dept.organisation.type.country

The **http://** is not normally typed into the address bar of the browser as, these days, it gets added automatically by the software. Frequently companies do not even mention it when displaying it in advertisements or on their carrier bags. It stands for "HyperText Transfer Protocol" and is the method used to send the web page files over the Internet. There are other protocols used for other kinds of data movement around the Internet and these have their own prefix. Increasingly, these are being ignored in newspapers, magazines and on television. For example, you rarely see the "mailto:" portion of the URL for an e-mail address.

A company's computer may be used for several different purposes on the Internet. The **dept** code portion of a URL is frequently used to indicate the part of the computer that serves its web pages and is almost always "www". However, it does not have to include "www" and occasionally you may find something else, or even no dept code at all. For example, Independent Television News displays its URL as "itn.com" on the closing credits of its broadcasts. Whilst this makes it short and snappy, it does create a small problem when entering the URL in the address bar, explained later.

The **organisation** code is, unsurprisingly, the name of the body that owns the site. Taken together with the next two parts of the URL, it is known as the Domain.

The **type** code describes the nature of the organisation. For commercial businesses this will normally be "com" or "co". The country in which the URL is registered determines which it is. Those registered in the UK will have "co" in the address, while those registered in the United States will be a "com". Some countries do not organise their domain names in this way and do not incorporate a type code in their domain names. If you look on the boxes of Kellogg's cereals you'll find that Ireland does not.

Except for the United States, the URL of the company's computer ends with a two-letter **country** code. As they invented the system, I suppose we can let them off not having to add a "us" to their addresses. As the web has developed, the effect of not having a country code has come to be interpreted by most people as "world-wide", so most large, and many aspiring, companies have tended to register their domains in the United States and become "dot com"s.

As you guess from these examples, each country has its own way of managing who gets the rights to a particular domain name. In the UK a body called Nominet maintains the register of the most popular of the domain types that the internet shopper is likely to see. These include:

>   co.uk - for commercial enterprises
>
>   org.uk - for non-commercial organisations
>
>   ltd.uk and plc.uk - for registered company names
>
>   net.uk - for Internet Service Providers

There are other UK domain types for personal use (me) or for government (gov) or other public bodies like the National Health Service (nhs), Ministry of Defense (mod), Schools (sch) other academic establishments (ac) and Police (police) forces, only some of which are managed by Nominet.

One trick worth knowing is that Internet Explorer will automatically add the http:// if you start by typing "www." in the address bar, so there is no need to add that bit. The downside to this is that it won't add it for those more rare addresses that do not start this way and, normally, it will go into "search mode" instead. This produces the problem, mentioned earlier, with an address like "http://itn.com"

A related trick is that, if the CTRL key is held down when hitting the carriage return key or when the "Go" button is clicked, Internet Explorer will automatically add an "http://www." prefix and a ".com" suffix to whatever has been typed in the address bar, making it very easy to change "marksandspencer" into:

http://www.marksandspencer.com

One further point on guessing a URL... Many companies register more than one. If you do enter "www.mands.co.uk", you'll be redirected automatically to Marks and Spencer's correct site.

Extended URLs

Sometimes URLs are extended with additional components. For example, the BBC has an extremely large web site and you rarely see it advertised in the form:

www.bbc.co.uk

Usually, it has a "/folder" after it. As this suggests, it simply indicates the folder in which the required web pages are filed on the computer. As with your own filing system on your hard disc, there can be several levels, so it is possible an address will be extended further, e.g. /folder/sub-folder/.

When any URL is entered into a browser, the computer will attempt to connect to the other computer indicated in the URL. Where the URL indicates only a particular computer system, or folder within a computer system, then a default file will be "served". Typically, this file will be called "index.html", "default.htm" or some variation on this theme.

If you do not want the default file sent to you from the specified computer or folder on that computer, then you can request a particular file from a named folder on that system. For example this URL, for a fictitious consumer affairs radio programme called "Your Problems", might take you to a page that lists presenters' addresses:

www.bbc.co.uk/radio4/yrprobs/contacts.html

You'll rarely be invited to type in a URL as long as this, so on the radio you'll normally just be told to "Go to the Radio 4 web site at www.bbc.co.uk/radio4, click on 'Your Problems' and find the 'Contact Us' button". However, if you allow your pointer to hover over the "Contact Us" button, the status line will indicate the full URL of the page that will appear on your screen, and this will take this form.

Internet Explorer's Search Facilities

Internet Explorer has two facilities built into it that help you find material on the Internet.

If you start to type something into the address bar of Internet Explorer that does not begin with "http://" or "www." then it assumes that you are attempting to search for a web page that includes the words that you are typing. As you type, a panel appears beneath the address bar that indicates a search being initiated.

If you do not complete the entry by holding down the Control key, to complete and initiate a request for a "dot com" URL, then Internet Explorer passes what you have typed to Microsoft's, "MSN Search" and a Results page will appear in the browser window:

MSN Home | My MSN | Hotmail | Shopping | Money | People & Chat
msn.co.uk

msn Search   Home | Advanced Search | My Preferences | Submit a Site | Help | Web Directory

cotton socks   [Search]

Results 1-15 of about 127733 containing "**cotton socks**"   NEXT >>

SPONSORED SITES - ABOUT
Buy Cotton Socks at Hawkshead
Hawkshead is trusted for quality, value and outdoor clothing that has stood the test of time. Every Hawkshead item comes with a no-nonsense guarantee.
www.hawkshead.com

Buy Cotton Socks at CTshirts.co.uk
Buy formal and casual shirts, shoes and accessories for men, women and children for all occasions. Buy online today and take advantage of 1993 prices for a limited time only.
www.ctshirts.co.uk

WEB PAGES - ABOUT
Mens **Socks** from EshopOne
A complete range of mens **socks** from EshopOne and wolsey. ... King Size **Socks. Cotton** Sock. Sports **Socks** ...
www.eshopone.com/smxhome/wolsey-socks

Falke **Cotton** Superfine **Socks** - Funky Colours from My Tights
SALE - DISCONTINUED PRODUCT. Fabulous short **cotton socks** from Falke in all the bright colours you can imagine. ... What do you get when you mix comfortable **cotton socks** with fluorescent paint? ...
www.mytights.com/mytights/1557.html

MSN Search is one of a number of web sites known as "search engines". We look at these in some detail in a later chapter. However, before examining them, it is worth noting the second built-in search facility in Internet Explorer.

In our tour of Internet Explorer we found the Search Button on the Standard Toolbar. If you click on this, a panel opens on the left of the browser window. This allows you to conduct exactly the same search that could have been conducted using the address bar. The only difference is in the way the results are presented.

Initially, the panel opens with the "Find a Web page" option selected. After entering the text, as before, a click on the "Search" button will bring up the list of results. This time the list is displayed in the panel and the main window shows "thumbnails", miniature images, of the top six sites from the results list. These thumbnails and the descriptions under them are links to the sites themselves.

Note that in this presentation of the results, there is no indication of the total number of pages that MSN Search has found. (Using the original method, the results screen indicated that MSN Search knew of almost 128,000 pages that included the words that had been entered!) Also, in this version, only twelve sites are listed in the panel instead of an initial fifteen, though in both versions, if you scroll down to the bottom, a "Next" link is found that will take you to see more. Curiously, MSN search only

shows thumbnails for the top six results shown in the panel, so if a site happens to be listed in the second six in any group, it will not get a thumbnail displayed, so don't just rely on the "pretty" thumbnails when thinking about what to click on to visit.

Web Searching – Some History

Having said earlier that experts would "use a search engine", it's worth providing a little background. Shortly after the web was first created, some people began to try to visit and classify as many sites as possible, listing them in a huge directory of web sites. A number of different teams, each with a different focus, produced their own directories. The task was already too big for one team and no one has ever succeeded in listing all available sites.

Listing, in those early days, was a totally manual process, involving a team of people examining sites, one by one, and deciding whether to include them in their directory and how to classify them. Later developments allowed users to enter key words into a form on the directory site and produce lists of pages from the directory that matched the user's key words. This made it much easier to find sites on topics that might cross over some of the section headings and sub-headings of the directory's classifications.

Meanwhile, before the Internet was a public medium and was still restricted to the military, government and academic communities, it was clear that the Web was becoming too big for manually searching out sites and classifying them. A number of university projects were started that attempted to classify web sites automatically. They used "crawler", also known as "spider", software that was programmed to find and list pages that had external links and then to follow those links to find other pages. Further software processes would then read the pages found and analyse their contents. With this information stored, it was then possible for users of these web sites to query the data, through a simple form, and obtain lists of pages that contained the desired terms. It was these "mechanised" sites that became known as "search engines" and they have largely replaced web directories for specialised searches.

Now that the web has grown so large it has become impossible to include all the known, or even worthwhile, sites within a directory structure. At some point, in a modern web directory, you may well have to enter some search terms on a form to get to select a sufficiently small number of pages to go through manually, or to get a precise enough selection of possible pages.

In the end, the only thing that sets the search engine apart from a web directory is that the process is completely machine driven, with no humans involved in the classification of sites or their retrieval from the lists of pages known to the engine.

In the early days of search engines, classification relied on hidden text, which authors included in their pages, held inside "meta-tags". As the power of computers increased and storage became cheaper, it became possible to classify pages on the basis of not just the text inside the meta-tags, but all the text on the page. While this means that it has become possible to find a page that matches, very closely, your requirements, it also means that it has become more important for the user to understand how to construct a search that will bring useful results.

As might be expected, in an academic environment, there was much competitive pride taken in ensuring the relevance and accuracy of search engine results. When, in the early 1990s, the Internet became a public medium, some of these university projects moved out of academia and a number became commercial enterprises, receiving revenue from advertisers. For a time there was some concern from users about whether search engine listings were being corrupted with advertiser's sites being listed higher in the results than would be justified according to the search terms selected. Now the market has matured, most reputable search engines clearly distinguish between those results that are paid for and those that have been listed solely on the basis of the search terms used. However, as with some magazine articles, the reader sometimes needs the "Advertisers Announcement" message to recognise the difference!

Web Searching – Now

Earlier it was explained how Internet Explorer has an automatic link to Microsoft's MSN search engine. In the following section Yahoo and Google are used to illustrate the use of web directories, rather than their search engine facilities. These days, these three, along with AllTheWeb, form what might be thought of as the "Big Four" amongst search tools. There are others, such as Alta Vista, AOL Search, Ask Jeeves, HotBot and Lycos and the URLs for all these are given in Appendix 1. There are, in fact, many more, but they tend to specialise in more limited fields and are less likely to be of interest to those only seeking banking and shopping sites. Some brands of search engine do not keep their own database of web sites but "buy in" results from another company. AOL Search makes no bones about this with a "powered by Google" banner. Look closely on some other sites and you'll see indications that they too buy in at least some of their results. This includes the BBCi's search facility.

Just as each web directory's editors will make different selections and choices, so each search results provider has its own suite of programs working to rules that are closely guarded commercial secrets. Many searches produce tens of thousands of "hits". What distinguishes a good search engine from a poorer one is which one lists useful pages early in the list. How they achieve this is not the concern of this book, though it is an interesting study of its own.

Summary

In many ways this chapter introduces the most important ones in the book. If a few months after going on-line you are still finding yourself forced to turn to magazines or books with titles like "Web Site Monthly" or "World's Best Web Sites 2002" as your only way of getting to the things you want to buy, then you cannot really consider yourself an effective Internet shopper.

If you have a hobby or passion that is even slightly out of the ordinary then you will find that it will not be covered in the general web site press.   It's true that these days most magazines covering specialist topics do recognise that many of their readers are "on-line", and do give references to web sites for further reading and places to buy the items referred to in the articles.   However, to get the best out of the Web, you will need to understand web directories and search engines, which are covered in the next two chapters and which offer the keys to effective Internet searching.

9

Using a Web Directory

The Web Directory Problem

The previous chapter explained that a Web Directory is a web site compiled by human editors that classifies and lists those sites that are expected to be of use to the directory's intended audience. Many would argue that now that the web has grown so large the web directory has had its day and that a Search Engine is a more effective tool.

That is probably true. However, "intended audience" is a key part of the definition of a web directory. While mass audience directories are losing their effectiveness for many searchers, if you fit in the target group, those with a highly specialised intended audience are still probably very effective sites to use.

To illustrate some of the issues, this chapter looks at a couple of the largest mass audience directories, Yahoo and Google, and attempts to find a source for a simple everyday item to buy. Further major directories are listed in Appendix 1.

An additional problem with web directories for UK-based on-line shoppers is that most are compiled with an American audience in mind. That means that the goods will be priced in US dollars and, frequently, there will be a lack of consideration of shipping costs to the UK. It can be a frustrating time, searching for somewhere suitable with whom to do business.

The Yahoo Directory

Yahoo is different to most directories. It was launched in 1994 and is the web's oldest. Like many sites it tries to capitalise on its popularity by taking advertising. This gives its home page a very cluttered tabloid magazine look, but this can be an advantage for the Internet shopper, who may wish to use the site as a multi-product brochure.

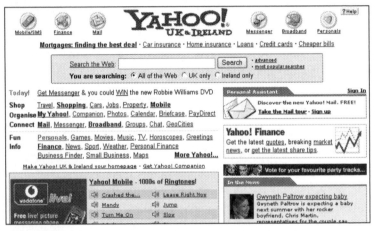

Yahoo UK: The top of the home page has a host of links and adverts. Scroll down to see the main directory categories

In the late 1990s, a lot of directory sites attempted to reposition themselves in the market and become "web portals", doorways to the Internet, from where you could launch any surfing session. Users were encouraged to make such sites their browser's home page. However, ISPs saw the threat and responded by establishing links with search providers, largely removing the appeal of the Directory based portal.

More important, perhaps, for a UK audience is that Yahoo does have a version aimed specifically at users in the UK and Eire:

http://uk.yahoo.com

If you've previously seen Yahoo's main site (http://www.yahoo.com) then, initially, you may not notice the differences. But a second look will make you realise this version refers to cars, not autos, and property, not real estate. There are further subtle differences that need not concern us here, but may be useful if you are searching for things other than your shopping requirements.

Yahoo's home page is a typical portal. It has a host of features intended to make it an attractive starting point for a web browsing session. Many of the links are designed to take you to pages promoting advertisers' products. The result is that it has a very cluttered appearance with such a mess of links that it can be hard for a newcomer to make out the best place to go next. However, for those who are looking for something to buy, a click on the bold "Shopping" link, just below the "Search the Web" box near the top of the page, takes you to its dedicated shopping home page that you can also get to directly by typing this into the address bar:

http://uk.shopping.yahoo.com/

The Shopping Home Page is only slightly less cluttered than the main page. The first thing you'll notice is a tabbed bar across the top of the page indicating different shopping areas, with a final tab offering further selections. You'll find that this bar is a static feature of Yahoo's Shopping area.

Under this header bar is a selection of specially promoted items. Buried much further down, under a host of adverts and trailers for other sections of the site is the main menu for Yahoo UK's shopping zone. A much "cleaner", almost advert-free version of this same menu can be found by clicking the "see more categories" tab at the top of the page.

On a normal web directory, and this includes Yahoo's main directory, you'll find that each of these main categories will take you to a further page, with a similar menu, that offers further subcategories until, several layers down, you reach a page that has a list of web pages that provide details of the products in which you are interested.

**The Yahoo Shopping "see more categories" page.
The "Hampers and Wine" option suggests that this menu,
seen in December, will change with the seasons**

You'll sooner discover that Yahoo's Shopping site is restricted to household and personal items only. There are other separate sections of the Yahoo site that cover shopping for holidays (travel), cars, jobs, property and even mobile phones. Each of these has its own colour-coded bar with sub-categories on it, though none of these leads you to the conventional menu of sub-categories. Instead, you will normally need to complete an on-line form, filling in boxes or selecting options from lists, to request details of the product for which you are searching.

If you are looking for something beyond the scope of the main headings in the Shopping directory you may be better off in the main Yahoo Directory. Although you can find the main directory headings listed on the site's portal page, you may find the clean advert-free version a more pleasing starting point. This is most easily reached from the portal by

clicking the "Search the Web" link in the search bar at the top of the page.

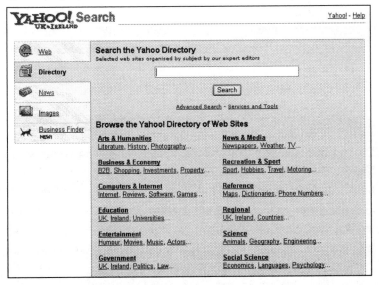

The advert-free version of Yahoo UK's Directory page is at:
http://uk.search.yahoo.com/search/ukie/dir/index.html

121

Selecting this innocuous text link moves you away from the wild commercialism of the rest of the site to the plain Yahoo Search page. This has a selection of "tabs" that lead you to pages that allow you to make five distinct types of search. The top tab, "Web" takes you to the true Search Engine, whose use is described in the next chapter. If you are going to use the directory, then select the second one down the list. The final tab, "Business Finder" may also prove invaluable for the internet shopper, as this is, in effect "Yellow Pages", as indicated by its URL!

Example Search

I decided to look at Yahoo UK's Shopping section for somewhere to buy some cotton socks. I started to drill my way down through the menus. However, I didn't get further than clicking the "clothing and accessories" tab, before I discovered that, on Yahoo, this leads you nowhere! The directory stopped at this level, with a cluster of advertisements for an assorted collection of feminine undergarments. To go further, and find what I was looking for, I had to enter the item I wanted in the search box:

Once I did this and clicked the "Search" button I was sent to a page that does, indeed, list a number of suppliers of cotton socks and these are listed in a way that is only found in the shopping section of the Yahoo site: "Found 34 products in 6 stores".

Further features of the site are useful if the list of stores is significantly longer than shown in this example. You can sort the results in various ways and, via the "Narrow your Search" panel on the left, you can select from the existing results by price or department.   In this "cotton socks" example, which may provide different results by the time you try it, it can be seen that there are 19 different products found between £5-£18 and that one of the products is likely to be of a novelty nature, as it had been classified under "Gifts" in the Yahoo directory, rather than "Clothing and Accessories".

The results of searching for "cotton socks" at the Yahoo UK Shopping site, with a mystery 11 products classified as neither "Gifts" or "Clothing and Accessories"

Google

Finding the right area in Google is slightly more difficult, even when logging onto the UK version of its site at:

http://www.google.co.uk

From the home page you may think it's a simple matter of clicking on "Directory" then "Shopping". However, do that and you'll find yourself in the US version of its shopping directory, as the first sub-heading, "Autos", gives away! To find the UK directory you first have to click the link to "Europe" under the "Regional" heading link. From there, you can find the "United Kingdom" section, and then its "Shopping" section.

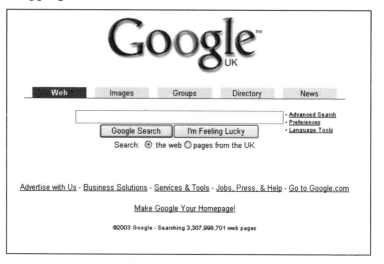

Google has a wonderfully uncluttered home page!
Click on the Directory tab to find its Web Directory

This is a useful example, as it does demonstrate both the classic way to navigate a directory and the problems such a system introduces. It is easy enough to start at the top level of the directory and work your way down through a series of headings and sub-headings until reaching the list of pages that provides you with the desired information.

It also demonstrates the problem of trying to find the pages you require if you are not thinking in the same way as the directory compiler. It may appear reasonable to an American compiler to have UK Shopping under a general European heading, but to a user, who has entered the Google's site via the UK home page then it might not occur to you that when you switch to the Directory section you have moved to the US site and need to navigate your way back to the UK before looking for the desired topic.

Google™
Directory

| Web | Images | Groups | **Directory** | News |

Google Search   • Preferences
• Directory Help

The web organized by topic into categories.

Arts
Movies, Music, Television,...

Home
Consumers, Homeowners, Family,...

Regional
Asia, Europe, North America,...

Business
Industries, Finance, Jobs,...

Kids and Teens
Computers, Entertainment, School,...

Science
Biology, Psychology, Physics,...

Computers
Hardware, Internet, Software,...

News
Media, Newspapers, Current Events,...

Shopping
Autos, Clothing, Gifts,...

Games
Board, Roleplaying, Video,...

Recreation
Food, Outdoors, Travel,...

Society
Issues, People, Religion,...

Health
Alternative, Fitness, Medicine,...

Reference
Education, Libraries, Maps,...

Sports
Basketball, Football, Soccer,...

World
Deutsch, Español, Français, Italiano, Japanese, Korean, Nederlands, Polska, Svenska, ...

Take care! Even though you may have started at Google UK the Directory tab takes you to the US version!

Example Search

At Google, I already knew that to get to the UK shopping directory I had to go via the Regional and European links, now I pressed on through "Shopping" and "Clothing", but then I came to a full stop. There were some 15 sub-sections under clothing but the closest two categories were "Footwear", which contained only boots and shoes and

"Natural Fibre" which contained a variety of companies selling knitwear, mainly in specialised wools.

However, one of the features of the Google directory is that every page lists a selection of related categories under which the items you seek may also have been classified.

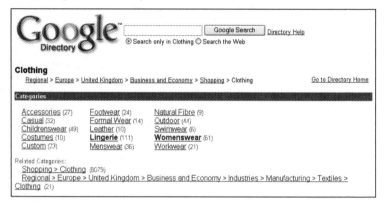

In this case these included two other categories of clothing, one, buried deep within the UK section, under textile manufacturing and the other within the main US shopping section. On moving to the American section of the directory, I found a different collection of sub-categories. These included an "Undergarments" section, within which was a specific "Socks and Hosiery" category, which listed over 90 sites.

By default, the Google Directory lists sites in "PageRank" order. Page ranking is a complex issue, which is examined further in the following section on Search Engines, but can be summarised as an attempt to place highest on the list the site likely to be most useful. Each entry has a coloured bar beside it which shows its ranking. In this case Google had found it difficult to distinguish between the entries and many appeared to have a similar ranking.

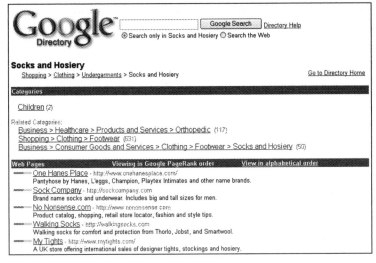

As is typical of Google, and in marked contrast to Yahoo's approach, the final results are displayed with limited, if any, commercial hype. Apart from the site name all that appears below each entry is a simple one-line description of the site.

In spite of this being the main directory listing, you will see that UK based companies are listed here, amongst the top ranking group of sites in the category.

If you get to this point in your search, where a long list of pages rather than further sub-categories are listed, and you now wish to search for companies you know, then it may be easier to click the link to sort the list into alphabetical order, rather than scroll through a long list, searching for names you recognise.

Conclusion

These two example searches have demonstrated the main problems with the use of directories:

127

- No one directory provides the best answers all the time.

There is no "Best" web directory. However, some general guidelines can be offered...

- When looking for mass market items the mainstream directories can be very effective tools.

Yahoo and Lycos both have advertised on television in the past and are therefore likely to offer a better choice for mass-market items.

- You must be prepared to think laterally.

It really pays to spend some time to become familiar with your chosen directory. Initially, it will frequently be necessary to start again from the very top list of categories and work down a completely different route to reach the kind of site you require.

- In the end, you may need to enter specific search terms and click a "Search" button to find what you require.

For more specialist items you need to find a specialist directory or use a search engine.

Using a
Search Engine

First Steps

Using a search engine is as simple as entering a few words that you would like to see on the web pages for which you are searching, clicking a button, then selecting and opening a page from the list that the search results screen provides. That's the theory! In practice to get the best out of a search engine requires a little understanding of how they work.

Many people turn to one of the big three search engines for their regular day-to-day searching, Google, Yahoo, and MSN Search. However, for shopping from UK-based sites you should make sure that you are using the UK version of the site.

If you are looking for something outside your normal range of purchases and your usual engine is not finding the right sites, then check with another. But don't pick the first one that comes to mind! Try to find one that does not buy in search results from the same provider as your current engine, otherwise although the results may be presented a little differently they are essentially from the same list. Remember, if you do turn to a new search engine, that it may use a slightly different syntax for the more complex searches, and be prepared to use its help facility.

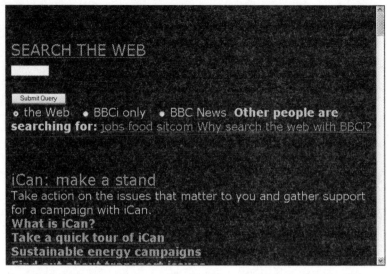

The text-only version of the home page of the BBCi site.
The user can set text size, colour scheme and font
from the link at the bottom of the page

The BBCi site may prove particularly welcome for users from the older generation as many have problems with their sight. It offers a special version of its search facility, and indeed its whole site, for those with visual impairment. This is provided through BETSIE, the "BBC Education Text to Speech Internet Enhancer". Not only is it designed for the blind, who may listen to the web through text-reading software, it also offers customisation of the font, size of text and colour scheme. This goes beyond the facilities that are offered when using Internet Explorer. Visit the BBCi site at:

http://www.bbc.co.uk

and look for the "Text only" link. The nearest equivalent to this may be AltaVista's "text-only search" at:

http://www.altavista.com/web/text

but this is only available in the US version of the directory, even though the UK version of the site apparently points to a UK version and provides UK based sponsored links.

Text Only Settings Page:

You can change the text-only settings by selecting from the following links. Select the last link when you are done.

Alternatively, select this link to return to the default settings.

Colours:

Yellow On Black , Black On White , White On Blue , Black On Cream

Font Size:

Tiny , Small , Medium Small , Medium , Large , Extra Large , Extra Extra Large

Font:

Verdana , Times , Courier , Helvetica , Arial , Bookman Old Style , Geneva , Chicago , Courier New , System

Notes:

Not all browsers support all possible font, size and colour combinations.

Most browsers allow you to specify your own font, size and colour combinations, overriding any given by the current page. You may find that route more flexible than the options allowed here. Consult your browser documentation for details.

Select this link when done

**The BETSIE page at the BBCi site
used for personalising the settings for the site**

Most of the results from the BBCi site come from the well-respected Google engine but it customises them, giving priority to sites "relevant to people living, working and studying in the UK". As with other BBC services funded through the licence fee, it is also completely free of advertisements and sponsors' announcements.

The Basic Search

All search engines have a box similar to the one here, primed to search for "cotton socks":

Alongside the field where you enter the required terms will be a button to initiate the search. Apart from "Search", this might be labelled "Go", "Find it", or even "Ask" in Ask Jeeves' case. Expect to find a "Help" link near this input box or at the top of the page. If you aren't getting the results you want, use it! One of the problems with both computers and the Internet is that things change all the time. Help that appears on-line at the search engine is likely to be more up to date than this book.

Another link that you will find nearby is almost certain to be labelled "Advanced Search". Don't be put off by this name. It certainly should not be taken to be for experienced users only. In fact, it might be better to call it "Complex Search for Beginners". There's a section that explains why later in the Chapter.

Any further options and links will vary according to the engine selected. The one illustrated at the start of this section comes from the UK and Eire version of Yahoo's main portal page (http://uk.yahoo.com.). This accounts for being able to set options to search "All of the Web", "UK only" and "Ireland only". Shoppers may well want to limit their searches to the UK because of worries about buying abroad,

132

currency exchange rates and so on. Other concerns about buying abroad are discussed in the final chapter.

Choosing Search Terms

Getting good results from a search engine is a matter of choosing the right terms. The first piece of advice is never search on a single word. Most words can be used a number of ways and the engine has no way to determine the right general area. For example, enter "blues" in most search engines and all the early results in the tens of thousands listed will assume that your interest is in music. However, you may be thinking of your daughter's post-natal depression or your favourite football team. It is also equally bad practice to list as many similes as possible, as is explained later when discussing the use of alternative terms.

As I mentioned "football" don't forget that the majority of English language web sites are created with an American audience in mind, so you might find a search on "soccer" gets you better results, as that's what the Americans call our national game. Similarly, remember that biscuits are cookies to Americans, and if you want to find American sites don't forget to try all those different spellings that Americans use.

Generally the more words you enter as search terms the better. Obviously, the more precise you are about the words that you expect to see on your ideal target page, the better is the chance that you'll be presented with a manageably small selection of pages in the results list, and that the results will, indeed, accurately reflect your requirements.

Counteracting the general advice that "more is better", you also need to choose your chosen terms carefully. Some will make no difference to your search and others may exclude significant numbers of appropriate pages. Words like "site", "web", "on-line", "buy", "store" and "shop" are taken by some search engines as "Stop Words". That is they are so common, occurring on so many pages, that they are discarded before the engine begins to search its records. In such cases there is no point in adding them to your search terms. Others, particularly adjectives, can have many synonyms and you may pick one that half of the potentially interesting sites have chosen not to use. So consider avoiding words like "olive" or "giant" when the more general "green" or "large" might do.

Once you have a number of suitable terms, also consider their order carefully. Entering "pink cotton socks" produces different results to "socks cotton pink" and different again with "socks pink cotton"! Place the more important terms early in the list with those that provide the context or add detail last.

Finally, be careful with capitals! In general, it is better to search using lower-case letters throughout. A number of search engines are case sensitive and will only match words with the same capitalisation as those that were presented to it. You'll need to check the "Help" page of the search engine you are using to decide if it applies to your chosen tool.

Searching for Phrases

Sometimes just having both words occur somewhere on the page is not good enough. They have to be next to each other and in the right order. In other words you need to search for an exact phrase. To get a particular phrase in the results in any of the search engines mentioned in this book simply enter the words between quote marks:

"cotton socks"

If you do try a search for "cotton socks" (in quotes) you may realise that this isn't just something I was trying to buy. I picked the phrase because I had known it, since childhood, as part of the expression, "Bless your little cotton socks!" It emerges that according to one American dictionary of phrases, it originated in 1905, though it doesn't record why cotton or why socks!

Avoiding Unwanted Results

Often you will find that results come up with inappropriate pages mixed in with good ones. To remove pages from the results that have unwanted terms in them include those terms in the search but prefix each of them with a minus sign. In all the major search engines this will get rid of virtually all these unwanted entries.

For example, if you haven't realised that you are using an American engine to search for books on postnatal depression and enter "baby blues" you will probably find that you have over three million hits and discover that there is a cartoon strip of that name. Scan the first page you see that almost half the results seem to relate to it and the words "cartoon" and "comics" appear a lot.

Re-run the search but with the words "comics" and "cartoon" added and prefixed with a minus sign, like this:

baby blues -cartoon -comics

Instantly, this clears the list of over a million hits. Incidentally, had the "baby blues" part been enclosed in quotes the number of hits drops to an almost manageable, by comparison, sixty thousand!

Searching for Alternative Terms

Having earlier advised you to use more terms rather than less, you shouldn't list a number of terms for the same thing. Take terms like "scent" and "perfume" or the phrases "B and B" and "Guest House". It is quite possible for web site creators to describe their products or services exclusively using only one term and not the other in the pair.

If you enter both the paired terms your search is likely to miss the sites that only use one of the pair. This is because most search engines will only return pages that match ALL the terms you submit. This is known as an AND based search and, these days, all the major search engines use this approach unless you specify otherwise. The problem with the alternative OR based search is there is not a standard way of asking for one term or another without both.

One solution is to look up the engine's Help pages, but if you plan to execute a search where you need an OR, it is often quicker to move to the "Advanced" search option and let the engine enter the correct method itself.

The Advanced Search

Close to the box for entering your terms into the search engine you are likely to find an "Advanced Search" link. As already explained, you should think of it as "Complex Search for Beginners". Visit an Advanced Search page and you will find many more boxes to fill in, but all these extra boxes are optional and designed to help you get more accurately targeted hits.

Ask Jeeves is a rare example of a search engine that hides its advanced search options well! In fact it doesn't brand its advanced search facility under the Ask Jeeves name at all. It bought the company Teoma, and through links on its help pages you can find you way to that engine's advanced search page. It's better to go there direct!

http://s.teoma.com/AdvancedSearch

The Ask Jeeves' advanced search retains the Teoma name

Usually, at the top of the page, you will find a direct replacement for the standard search engine input box, labelled "All these words", the AND search. Grouped with this will be others. Sometimes they'll be a set of boxes specifically labelled. On others, as with Teoma, drop-down lists allow the boxes to be converted for a variety of purposes. However it is presented, there will be a method for entering an exact phrase, which does the same job as adding the quotation marks round the words when entered in the standard search box. A "None of these words" or "Must not have" box or option is the equivalent of the one that places minus signs in front of the terms and hence excludes them from pages listed in the results. Another, typically labelled either "Any of these words", "At least one of these words" or "Should have" does the job of providing an OR search. If you find that you are not sure where to add quotation marks, minus signs and so on, then the Advanced Search will be especially helpful. Take care though, for it is also easy to add many further pages to the results, without any more relevance to your needs.

Returning to the football example briefly, searching for both football AND soccer may well produce results that include many sites produced by fans of the game, as they are more likely to use both words, whereas the official club sites may well avoid the use of the word soccer, referring to football only.

Assuming that you are not searching at a "UK only" version of the search engine, a search on football OR soccer will probably introduce American based sites to the results, as they tend to use football to describe their own national game and will tend to use soccer without reference to football.

If you place the words football and soccer in both the "All the words" and "Any of the words" boxes, then you will be more likely to pick up both professional and amateur sites from both sides of the Atlantic on our game of football, along with references to American football as well. To stop references to American football you need to find a term that would exclude them and place that in the "None of these words" line. "NFL", the American "National Football

League", should work well. Adding "Football Association" or "FIFA" to the "Any of the words" line would also reinforce that the results should be about our game only.

On the AltaVista Advanced Search Page there is help with some of the individual fields as well as a general Help link

The remaining items on an advanced search page vary from engine to engine. For many searches they can be left at their default settings, but they all have their uses in removing unwanted results.

Language: Ideal for finding those French and German hotels and villas when planning a do-it-yourself holiday, rather than taking a package.

Where on page: These options will be rarely needed by the internet shopper, but are worth explaining for the other times when you may use a search engine. They tend to be presented a little differently by each search engine but usually include the following options:

- Title: This refers to the text on the title bar of the browser, the blue bar, with the standard colour scheme, at the top of the window.

- Text: The main body of the page, which includes any heading and titles you might see there.

- URL: The address of the page. Many sites use quite English words as folder names. The BBC is a good example, with folders labelled history, news, education, antiques, lifestyle and so on. Entering a set of brand names in the "Any of these words" box and selecting them to be found in the URL is a good way of finding small-scale enterprises that sell those goods. Whilst many large on-line retailers have complex sites that build the pages dynamically according to options chosen by the visitor, smaller businesses tend to have fixed sites with sections for different parts of their business. These sections are often held in different folders. Picking a common brand name or product type may well be a way of targeting small business sites that sell those products.

- Links: Useful if you want to contact related businesses. If you haven't heard of a web site, but they seem to have something in stock that you want, you could try searching for their name in links. This should bring up a list of sites that have some business relationship with them and are prepared to name and link to them from their own site. Seeing some names you recognise amongst the results of the search may be enough to tip the balance in deciding whether to use them or not. Many manufacturers will list the sites of local stockists. Enter the name of a business and you might turn up one of their suppliers. You might be able to get a better price by buying direct, or the name of an alternative supplier if your chosen one is out of stock of the item you seek.

Site/Host /Domain/URL: These four terms, although related, are not interchangeable. To make matters difficult some engines use them to refer to slightly different things. You need to check, with the site's help or hints given on the page. The function, however, is always to limit the search. You may be able to limit it to just addresses that end in ".com" or ".co.uk" or even "uk", or to those addresses that contain a particular word or phrase somewhere in the middle of the address, or restrict the search to within a single web site by entering a complete address.

For example, if you know the company with whom you want to do business, then you could enter their web site address here in the appropriate box. The engine would then look for your search terms only within that site. This is good for looking for particular brands or particular goods at large sites that aren't organised in the way that seems logical to you. Alternatively, in the box for parts of addresses you could enter "camera" and not only would you get results for companies with an address like "www.camerasonline.co.uk" but also from large sites which had a section for cameras in a folder that included "camera". Finally, one could restrict the search to companies from the UK, though entering ".co.uk" would stop results from camera clubs which would typically end in ".org.uk".

Geographic: Many sites are written in English but are foreign. Use this filter to limit the pages retrieved in the results.

Date: There is debate about how good this criterion is for internet shoppers. Whilst it can be useful for searching for static information and historic or academic papers, it is not likely to be helpful for those buying through dynamically constructed shopping sites.

File Format: If you're buying the latest MP3 file to give to your grandchildren for their birthday (It's the new way of buying records!), then searching for a particular name and limiting the search to this file type is the thing to do. Similarly, books are increasingly being sold as electronic files, or "e-books", rather than as paper pages between hard or soft covers. Many of these are sold in PDF format. This is the format that is used for many computer manuals that are supplied on CD-ROM with the software that they describe. They have the great benefit that you can read them on screen with as much magnification as you need. If even large print books are not large print enough for you, then e-books may suit you, as you can usually print them in still larger print.

Adult Filter: If you are looking for underwear but get nothing but sex and pornography? Turn on the adult content filter!

Similar to: If you find a site that looks good then enter its URL here and the engine will analyse it and find other similarly indexed sites. It's simpler than trying to work out all the relevant key words yourself!

After entering all the criteria for the search and clicking the button to initiate the search, as before, a results page appears. The components of the results screen are examined in the next section. However, normally, at both the top and bottom of the page the standard search box appears, containing the search terms specified to obtain the displayed results. This will contain the terms from the multiple boxes of the advanced search screen reduced to a single line. The syntax of this line varies with the engine used. Examination of how it is constructed can allow you to build complex search instructions without use of the advanced search screen.

AltaVista is an exception as it does not display its standard search box on the results page but the same complex set of boxes that appear on the advanced search page. However, a Help page at:

http://www.altavista.com/help/adv_search/syntax

as seen on the next page, clearly describes the syntax.

True advanced users of search engines will learn the syntax of these lines, and be able to type it directly into the standard search box, rather than use the advanced search option. Intermediate users may choose to copy examples of the strings of search terms and paste them into a Notepad file kept for the purpose. It is then easy to open the file, select one of the saved search strings from the appropriate search engine, and with this reminder of the syntax, make the minor amendments needed for the current search. The amended string can then be pasted into the search engine's find box.

10 Using a Search Engine

Home > AltaVista Help > Search > Special search terms

You can use these terms for both basic and advanced Web searches. For advanced searches, type these into the free-form Boolean box.

AND	Finds documents containing all of the specified words or phrases. **Peanut AND butter** finds documents with both the word peanut and the word butter.
OR	Finds documents containing at least one of the specified words or phrases. **Peanut OR butter** finds documents containing either peanut or butter. The found documents could contain both items, but not necessarily.
AND NOT	Excludes documents containing the specified word or phrase. **Peanut AND NOT butter** finds documents with peanut but not containing butter. NOT must be used with another operator, like AND. AltaVista does not accept 'peanut NOT butter'; instead, specify **peanut AND NOT butter**.
NEAR	Finds documents containing both specified words or phrases within 10 words of each other. **Peanut NEAR butter** would find documents with peanut butter, but probably not any other kind of butter.
*	The asterisk is a wildcard; any letters can take the place of the asterisk. **Bass*** would find documents with bass, basset and bassinet. You must type at least three letters before the *. You can also place the * in the middle of a word. This is useful when you're unsure about spelling. **Colo*r** would find documents that contain color and colour.
( )	Use parentheses to group complex Boolean phrases. For example, **(peanut AND butter) AND (jelly OR jam)** finds documents with the words 'peanut butter and jelly' or 'peanut butter and jam' or both.
anchor:_text_	Finds documents that contain the specified word or phrase in the text of a hyperlink. **anchor:job +programming** would find pages with job in a link and with the word programming in the content of the page. Do not put a space before or after the colon. You must repeat the keyword to search for more than one word or phrase; for example, **anchor:job OR anchor:career** to find pages with anchors containing either the word job or the word career.
applet:_class_	Finds pages that contain a specified Java applet. Use **applet:morph** to find pages using applets called morph.
object:_class_	Finds pages that contain a specified object created by another program (eg. a Flash object). Use **object:money** to find pages using objects called money.
domain:_domainname_	Finds pages within the specified domain. Use **domain:uk** to find pages from the United Kingdom, or use **domain:com** to find pages from commercial sites.
host:_hostname_	Finds pages on a specific computer. The search **host:www.shopping.com** would find pages on the Shopping.com computer, and **host:dilbert.unitedmedia.com** would find pages on the computer called dilbert at unitedmedia.com.
image:_filename_	Finds pages with images having a specific filename. Use **image:beaches** to find pages with images called beaches.
like:_URLtext_	Finds pages similar to or related to the specified URL. For example, **like:www.abebooks.com** finds Web sites that sell used and rare books, similar to the www.abebooks site. **like:sfpl.lib.ca.us/** finds public and university library sites. **like:http://www.indiaxs.com/** finds sites about culture on the Indian subcontinent.
link:_URLtext_	Finds pages with a link to a page with the specified URL text. Use **link:www.myway.com** to find all pages linking to myway.com.
text:_text_	Finds pages that contain the specified text in any part of the page other than an image tag, link, or URL. The search **text:graduation** would find all pages with the term graduation in them.
title:_text_	Finds pages that contain the specified word or phrase in the page title (which appears in the title bar of most browsers). The search **title:sunset** would find pages with sunset in the title.
url:_text_	Finds pages with a specific word or phrase in the URL. Use **url:garden** to find all pages on all servers that have the word _garden_ anywhere in the host name, path, or filename.

Get the **AltaVista Toolbar**.

The Results List

Once the "Search button is clicked, the engine searches for pages that include the terms you provided and displays a list of "hits". It is not uncommon to be told that there are tens of thousands, sometimes millions, of these with, initially, the first ten displayed.

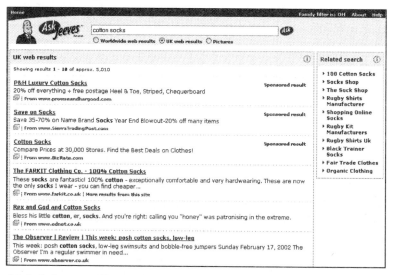

At Ask Jeeves the small overlapping window icon beside each result will open the link in a new window.
The screen also suggests further related searches

Exactly how the results are displayed will depend on the engine, with the calculation of the ranking of any page a commercially sensitive secret. The header of the results page will contain a copy of the search box, showing the terms entered. Usually, this is repeated in the footer of the page as well. These can be used to erase or edit the existing terms, useful if the original results are inadequate and a minor change will bring more appropriate results.

Yahoo shows sponsored results followed by the top 20 results, with unrelated advertisements to the right

Under the header on most search results screens will be a list of "sponsored links", though some display them to one side of the page. These links are, in effect, advertisements. The advertiser normally pays for a list of trigger words and the adverts are displayed when a user includes them in their search. The longer the list of triggers, the more searches are likely to display the advertisements, the more users click on the links and the more the advertiser pays.

The bulk of the page is taken with the listing of hits. There are normally three distinct parts to an entry. First, the page title is given, usually in bold in some bright contrasting colour and underlined. The page title is that part of the page which is normally displayed as the document name on the blue title bar of Internet Explorer. Under this will be a "quote" from the selected page. This should have a sprinkling of emboldened words matching the search terms.

The BBCi search results page has no advertising or sponsored links, so has a much less cluttered appearance

You use these first two elements of any "hit" to attempt to determine whether any page is likely to be one of interest to you. The final line, again often in a different contrasting colour, is normally the URL of the listed page. This is important if you choose to print the page of results, as it will be the only way to identify the URL of the page. The page title, and often the URL, will be displayed as links.

The BBCi text-only results screen prominently displays whether links are external to the BBC site. This can be helpful for those who know they will find it difficult to view the conventional graphics-laden pages of most sites. In spite of the BBC's claim to provide results "relevant to people living, working and studying in the UK" you may still need to use some advanced search techniques to rid the results of

American sites, as is evidenced in the search for "cotton socks"!

The BETSIE service at the BBCi site inserts a line space between the title and quote of each site's entry

The AltaVista text-only results page is more conventional. It relies on the user having customised their browser heavily to make significant changes in the appearance of pages. What it does provide is a page that lacks any advertisements, other than sponsored links. In spite of the name, it does retain a single logo graphic at the bottom of the page.

The final component of the results page, if your search has produced many hits, will be found just above the footer. This will be a set of links that lead you on to further pages of results. Typically this area will comprise "previous" and "next" links and a group of page numbers. Each of these will be a link to that page except, of course, for the number indicating the current page.

Pants & Socks - ... White sports **sock** with ?Bow Side? knitted into one **sock** in green and ?Stroke Side? in red on the other **sock**. 80%/20% **cotton**/polyester mix. Single pair. ...
http://www.rock-the-boat.co.uk/pages/Pants___Socks/pants___socks.html

1 2 3 4 5 6 7 8 9 10 next »

Targeted Searches
- Search eBay.co.uk to buy and sell "cotton socks"
- Find Kids Only sites about "cotton socks"
- Search for Books about "cotton socks"
- Find AOL Member Webpages about "cotton socks"
- Search Shop@AOL for "cotton socks"

More Searches
- Maps & Directions
- Kids Search
- Flight Finder
- Business Finder
- Local Info
- Job Finder

AOL Search POWERED BY Google™   cotton socks   Search   Advanced | Help
○ Whole Web ⦿ UK sites

About AOL Search | Add Your Site | Advertise With Us
Copyright © AOL (UK) Ltd. All rights reserved. Terms of Use

AOL makes it clear who provides its search results!
"Targeted Searches" offer a "Shop@AOL" feature

If you are lucky with your first searches, you will find pages that meet your requirements listed in the first page or two of the results list. The problem comes if your search fails to find anything suitable. You will need to consider why your results are not as hoped and either edit the terms in the search box appropriately and re-submit the search, or choose one of the other links found on the page, designed to help you refine your search. These are described in the next section.

Cotton Socks at Dealtime.com
Simplify your shopping with DealTime! Great Deals - **cotton socks** - DealTime is a service that makes comparing products, prices
stores ... **cotton socks** cottonsocks ccotton **socks** cootton **socks** ...
www.dealtime.com/xKW-COTTON_SOCK/kworg-C...2081972/GS.html

Result Pages: 1 2 3 4 5 6 7 8 9 10 Next >>

[Graphic Version]

altavista

Business Services   Submit a Site   About AltaVista   Help

© 2004 Overture Services, Inc.

There's no search bar at the bottom of the AltaVista text-only results. The graphics version offers to install a "toolbar" to encourage you to search again with them

Additional Features of the Results List

Depending on the engine there may be some further links associated with certain entries. For example, AltaVista, AOL Search, LookSmart and Yahoo all offer a "More pages from…" link, if other hits from the same site have been found. Showing only one page from a site and then placing a link to other relevant pages from that site is known as "clustering". Most search engines have such a feature turned on by default. With some engines it is possible to visit a preferences screen to undo the effect of this clustering.

Google UK shows related directory classifications at the top, in this case the US directory! It shows sponsored links to the right and clusters results from the same site

Google and others offer a "Similar Pages" search. Selecting similar pages re-submits the search with additional terms that have been found on the current page. This can be useful as a way of reaching the most likely candidates when faced with tens of thousands of results that have been taken by the engine to match your search terms. An alternative, used by some other engines, is an option to "Search within results", which allows you to add further terms to an existing search and thin the results down that way.

Google, uniquely, also offers a "Cached" link as well. Selecting the cached page does not take you to the true URL of the page selected, but instead takes you to the version of the page that was available at the time it was indexed and analysed by Google. With some pages, especially those that are updated very regularly, it is possible to find that, when visited, the page has no place on the results screen as it has no information relevant to the search terms. Visiting the cached page will show you the version that was available when the page was indexed. This version should be relevant to your search, even if the current version of the page is not.

Summary

There's more to using a search engine than typing in a few words. Choose your initial words and phrases to be as precise as possible. To refine the results, re-search adding terms to exclude unwanted pages, making sure you are using the engine's correct syntax.

Don't be put off from using the "Advanced Search" feature of search engines. They are better thought of as "Complex Search for Beginners".

If you can spare the time, do a practice search every time you go on-line! Don't get distracted with something fascinating that turns up along the way. The web can be very beguiling! Set yourself something to find and keep changing the terms you use and adjusting the syntax of your search command, even change engines, if necessary, until you can turn up some good results.

11

The Banking Process

From High Street to Internet

There is one thing that separates my banking habits over the last thirty years compared with my shopping habits. I can't remember when I last went in a bank!

Over the last thirty years, I have moved from house to house around the country, but the bank, and indeed the branch, that nominally held my account has remained the same. For years I used machines to get cash, but more recently have found that the supermarket's habit of offering me "cash back" supplies almost all my needs. When I needed a new cheque book I used to pop the request form from the back of my old one in the post. However, these days I rarely use cheques, as I have moved to using debit and credit cards.

When telephones stopped whirring and clicking as you dialled a number and started beeping at you instead, telephone banking was introduced. I used the service to set up and cancel direct debits and standing orders and arrange for those varying, but regular, payments to be made for such things as gas, electricity and the telephone. When I needed one, the occasional personal loan could be arranged by telephone too.

Then internet banking arrived. With internet banking I could do all that I did previously over the phone, but with the added confidence of being able to keep a record of each transaction.

Banking On-line

All the major banks now offer on-line banking to their customers and they all offer similar services. Perhaps, as someone young at heart, if not in years, part of the attraction of on-line banking is being able to take up with one of the new fancy on-line banks with a strange name, like "Egg", "Cahoots", "Smile" or "Marbles". More likely, you are just a little conservative and simply want to deal with your existing bank account.

You should expect an on-line bank to be able to allow you to:

- Order cheque and paying-in books
- Activate newly arrived credit cards
- Display and print all statements of account
- Download account data for import to your software
- Set up, amend and cancel standing orders
- Review and cancel direct debit instructions
- Set up and make bill payments
- Make transfers between accounts at the same bank
- Make transfers to accounts at another bank

Not all on-line banks offer all these services and their approaches are all slightly different. Besides allowing you to view account statements on-line, most will also allow you to download the data as a "CSV" file, or in other formats for particular software packages. A "comma separated values" file is a format that any spreadsheet program can handle and many other accounting packages too.

The rest of this chapter examines how you carry out some of these actions using the on-line facilities of two High Street banks. In fact, most banks have complete "walk-though" demonstrations available for potential customers to try out.

Logging on

More than any shopping site, banks are anxious to reassure you that your money is safe with them. So getting access to information about your account is a little more involved than checking out most shopping sites. Not only will you normally need a "username", NatWest call it a "Customer Number", but both a "password" and a PIN as well.

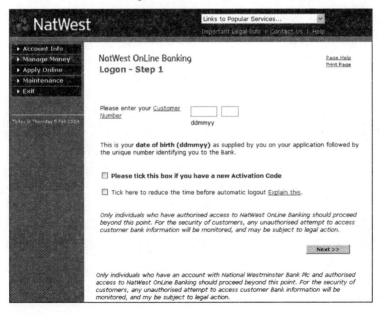

After entering the customer number on the first of the Logon screens, you then enter selected characters from both your password and PIN on the second screen.

NatWest OnLine Banking
Logon - Step 2

Page Help
Print Page

Please enter the fourth, third and first digits from your PIN:

Please enter the first, third and sixth characters from your Password:

<< Back   Next >>

The characters that are selected to enter on this screen vary at each logon. As with all passwords, the characters do not display on the screen. Only asking for a number of characters from your password does mean that even if someone sees the keys you press, they will have to be standing beside you several times before they manage to detect the full PIN or password.

After this screen, NatWest has been displaying a security notice about fraudulent emails purporting to come from the bank and asking recipients to post them passwords and other personal data. Warnings like this may not appear or be replaced from time to time. The "Next" button takes you to a further warning screen that reports the last time you logged on to the bank's site. This allows you to check that no one has managed to break into your account. You are instructed to exit the site and telephone the bank immediately, if you believe that this shows an incorrect date. Once you have clicked the next button on each of the warning screens, you are through to the account balances screen.

At the Lloyds TSB site logging on is very similar except that it uses the more conventional terms and rather than a PIN a second page asks for randomly selected characters from previously determined "Memorable Information":

Lloyds TSB online   ● Register now

Welcome to Internet banking

You are now in a secure area. Please keep your password confidential at all times. Always click Logoff after completing your banking and disconnect from the Internet before leaving your computer unattended. **Click here for further security information**

To log on enter your User ID and password.

User ID   [   ]

Password   [   ]   ● Continue

Forgotten User ID | Forgotten Password and Memorable Information | Help | LloydsTSB.com

The data held on Lloyds TSB host system is PRIVATE PROPERTY. Access to the data is only available for authorised users and purposes. Unauthorised entry contravenes the Computer Misuse Act 1990 and may incur criminal penalties as well as damages. Please proceed if you are an authorised user.

Lloyds TSB online   ● Register now

entering your **memorable information**   User Id / Password   Memorable Information   Logged on

To complete log on please enter the requested numbers and/or letters from your Memorable Information using the 3 drop down lists provided. Please click on 'Help' if you require further assistance.

Please enter characters 1, 4 and 7 from your memorable information

1 [▼]   4 [▼]   7 [▼]   ● Logon

Help | LloydsTSB.com

The two-stage Logon process at Lloyds TSB online

Account Lists and Details

Once through the logon procedure, the next screen to be seen typically will list the accounts that you hold and their balances. Some banks will provide further information. NatWest calls this screen "Account Balances and Mini-

11 The Banking Process

Statements". It includes a list of recent transactions for one of the accounts. Selecting another account from the list at the top displays the recent entries for that account instead.

The equivalent Lloyds TSB screen is called the "Account List" and holds less information than that of NatWest. It doesn't either list the available balance, which allows for cleared cheques, or have a snapshot of recent transactions.

The NatWest screen includes an "Edit Account Name" button. The ability to edit the name is useful as, by default, the field shows only the name, sole or joint, of the account holder. If your accounts have similar balances and you can't recall the account numbers, then a list of accounts with identical names is not helpful. At Lloyds TSB the ability to change the account name, or "Nickname" as Lloyds call it, is on the Account Details screen.

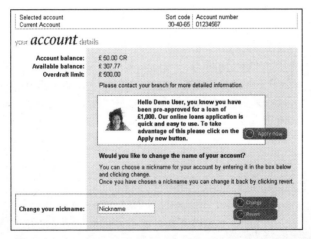

As you will already know, if you hold accounts at a number of different banks, each uses terminology slightly differently. For example, at Lloyds TSB clicking on "Account Details" on the menu at the left of the screen produces a screen that shows current information, such as the current and available balances and the overdraft limit. The "Account Details" screen at NatWest, on the other hand, shows historic information about the account, such as the account number, account type, branch details and date of opening.

NatWest OnLine Banking

Page Help
Print Page

Account Details

ACCOUNT NAME	My Current Account
ACCOUNT NUMBER	11111111
SORT CODE	601111
ACCOUNT DESCRIPTION	CURRENT ACCOUNT
BRANCH ADDRESS	NATWEST BANK 1 THE STREET ANYTOWN
DATE ACCOUNT OPENED	27 Feb 2000

<< Back

Statements

For many the principle reason for going on-line to do their banking is to check that their salary or pensions have been received and that there is sufficient money in their account to pay any bills that are due. Most on-line banks not only allow you to view a statement, but also allow you to download an electronic version which can then be imported into a spreadsheet or some more specialised financial package.

The NatWest site menu system, towards the top right of the window, reveals additional options when a main heading is clicked. Click on "Account Info" and options are displayed that enable you to return to the "Balances and Mini Statements" page or display or print bank account and credit card account statements. The "Transaction Search" option provides a means by which you can check back to see when a bill was paid or credit received.

Selecting "Statements" takes you to a screen that provides a default statement. The "Create New Statement" button on this screen allows you to select the period and account that you wish to see.

The "Download Statement" button moves you to the same screen that can also be reached from the main menu. This allows you to pick which accounts you wish to include in the download file, the period to be covered and the format of the file. Not all banks provide the same options for the file format of the download and if considering changing banks, this could be an important factor for the decision on which bank to which to move.

If your accounting package is not included in the list which NatWest provides then select the "CSV" option. CSV stands for "Comma Separated Values" and is a plain text format that is supported by a huge range of software packages, not just

11 The Banking Process

Microsoft's Excel and the Lotus 123 spreadsheet programs suggested by NatWest's list.

Lloyds TSB offers almost identical facilities, but because the menu structure is arranged a little differently you navigate to the option in a different way. For example, there is no "Statement Download" option on the main menu at the Lloyds TSB site. Instead, the pages that display the statements provide a drop-down list from which you can choose options to select a "Printer friendly statement" or one of two file format options.

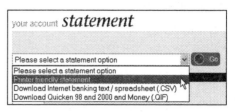

In contrast, at the NatWest site a printed statement is best obtained through the link that appears towards the top right of the page. The NatWest site has a similar, "Print page" link on virtually every page of the site. On any site always choose the "printer friendly" option in preference to the normal browser print facilities. This is because these options link to special versions of the pages that should exclude features, such as the menus and other material, not needed in a printed version, producing a much better document for filing with other financial records.

Transfers

After examining your current financial status, you may want to transfer money between accounts before making any payments.

At NatWest these processes are handled through options on the "Manage Money" section of the main menu. At Lloyds TSB you use the "Transfers and Payment" screen, reached from the link on the main menu. The options that appear on the main Lloyds TSB menu are not fixed, in the same way as those on the NatWest site, and this option does not appear until an account has been selected from the "your Account List" page.

Lloyds TSB offers no facility to set a date for a transfer between accounts and all transfers are made immediately. The screen shown above shows that this is not true for payments, which can be scheduled in advance. For those who plan their finances so that the maximum interest is being earned from any savings, and current account balances are kept to a minimum, it will be necessary to log on to the Lloyds TSB site every time a payment is due in order to make a transfer to cover the payment.

At NatWest you have the same option to schedule a transfer as you do with a payment. This means that you can both set a payment for a future date, and arrange a transfer from a savings account to a current account to cover it, without needing to log on when the payment is due – a much more satisfactory arrangement.

NatWest OnLine Banking

Transfer Money

Page Help
Print Page

Create Transfer

To amend or cancel, click on the relevant pending transfer.

DATE	STATUS	FROM ACCOUNT	ACCOUNT TO	AMOUNT
20 May 2003	Pending	My Current Account	My Savings Account	£100.00
15 May 2003	Pending	My Current Account	My Savings Account	£60.00
09 May 2003	Complete	My Current Account	My Savings Account	£275.00
08 May 2003	Complete	My Current Account	My Savings Account	£40.00

▲ back to top

NatWest OnLine Banking

Create Transfer

Page Help
Print Page

Select the accounts for the transfer together with the transfer amount and the date on which it should take place. Click Confirm to make the transfer.

From this account: My Current Account (£1456.48 available)

To this account: My Current Account (£1456.48 available)

Amount: £0.00

Payment Date: 10 May 2003

Confirm   Cancel

The first of these NatWest screens shows the schedule of transfers, the second where you create a new transfer

Payments

In contrast to transfers between accounts, the payment facilities offered by these two banks are very similar. In both cases, you first set up a list of possible payees, and then authorise payments that can be made either immediately or on a date that you set. Both banks distinguish between "bills" and "payments".

Both call the main household expenses "bills". The banks keep details of the principal suppliers of water, gas, electricity, local councils and so on and setting them up requires little more than entering the payee's name, or picking it from a drop-down list, and supplying a reference or account number.

Anything else is referred to as a "payment", "Third Party Payment" in the case of NatWest and "Payment to another person" if your account is with Lloyds TSB. In these cases, apart from picking the account to be charged, you will need to supply the name of the account to be credited, the sorting code and account number, and any reference that that payee might require to identify the payment, such as an invoice number or other note.

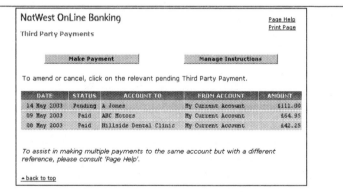

The NatWest Third Party Payment Screen: Amend and cancel payments here. Use the "Manage Instructions" button to add payees and "Make Payment" button to set an amount to pay

In both cases, once the details have been entered, you are returned to the main payments screens, which show the schedule of pending payments. In the case of Lloyds TSB the screen to which you are returned is the one already seen when discussing transfers, which lists both forthcoming bills and payments. NatWest keeps bills and payments separate, but offers the benefit of showing recently made transactions as well as pending ones.

Management

A crucial function of any on-line banking service is to help you keep your information secure. It is always regarded as good practice to regularly change items such as passwords and PINs. Options are provided to allow users to do this. The trouble, for us of the older generation, is that while it may be easy for us to remember things from half a century ago, we tend to forget things we did recently. This means that we are more likely to do one of the things we are encouraged never to do – write down these items. Unfortunately, the banks make it difficult by asking us to enter random characters from the middle of these passwords! It's much easier to work out which letter is which if we have it written down beside us as we log on.

 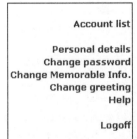

Whatever the problem, there is no doubt that regularly changing passwords and PINs does add a measure of security that is worthwhile, especially if you ever do any on-line banking away from your own computer at an Internet café or local library.

Applications

Banks are always after more business, so you can expect prominent links to related services on their web sites and you'll find them in the "Apply On-line" section. One of the great revolutions in the financial services sector over the last ten years has been the growth of the "buy it by telephone" market.

Where once you would have visited an insurance company office or independent broker to obtain the best deal, now the high street offices have closed and you by-pass the middleman and contact your chosen company direct. These companies continue to advertise their telephone services, but increasingly offer insurance on the Internet.

The "Apply Online" menus for the two banks.
NatWest seems to be missing a commercial trick here!

Banks too have expanded their range of services. It may be that your bank will now offer you not only the cheapest loans but insurance deals too. (If not, then use the techniques suggested in the earlier chapters to find a company offering the right product for you.)

Summary

The purpose of this chapter was not to provide a detailed guide to the on-line services of the two banks covered, but to illustrate the range of financial tasks that can be carried out on-line with any bank. A bank's web site is liable to change far more frequently than its logo, so do not expect things to be exactly the way I have presented them here when you come to read the book.

Internet banking offers many benefits, outstripping telephone banking through its ability to provide printed records of all transactions and instructions, and no local branch is able to provide the opening hours that telephone or internet banking offers.

There is no necessity to change banks to move to Internet banking. All the main banks offer on-line services. For most banks, all that you need to do is go to your bank's web site and register your intention to start using the service. The bank will then mail you any additional passwords or PINs that are required.

For day-to-day management of one's finances internet banking offers all that anyone would require. The various banks do provide differing peripheral on-line services, which may include insurance services, facilities for loan and credit card applications, requests for foreign currency, but for most people these will not crucially affect their choice of bank, and transfer to one of the new "Internet-only" banks is not required.

Internet banking is simple. While there are one or two things that may need getting used to, the difference between a "bill" and a "payment", for example, the actual process of transferring money between accounts, paying money, reviewing balances and forthcoming commitments is as simple as it gets.

Internet banking is secure. Yes, it is possible for things to go wrong, but so it is with any other part of life. Internet banking will always be a lot safer than collecting money from a high street cash machine, and you're never going to leave your cheque-book or credit card behind on some shop counter, when internet banking! There is no credible reason for refusing to become involved in internet banking on grounds of the security of your money.

The Buying Process

From High Street to Internet

As on the High Street where every shop is different, each one trying to carve its own niche in the market place, so too with internet shops. Why do you pick Tesco, over Waitrose, Sainsbury, Morrison or Aldi, to buy your groceries? It often isn't because it's the closest to home, but something to do with the brands they sell, the price, or something less tangible about the way they do business and the service they provide. Internet shopping is exactly the same. Contrary to popular opinion, internet shopping need not just be about finding the lowest price; it can be about service too!

Supermarkets all seem to work in exactly the same way these days. You grab a trolley, fill it, and pay for the goods at the checkout. Being of the older generation, you'll remember that grocery shops used to have staff that did more than stack shelves. Sainsbury's branches used to be small double-fronted shops. Each side of the store had long marble counters stretching all the way to the back of the shop, with staff waiting to serve you every few feet along the counter. I particularly loved watching the man cut the required portion of butter, perhaps just a couple of ounces, from a huge block. He'd pat it into shape with grooved wooden paddles, weigh it, write the price in blue pencil on a sheet of greaseproof paper and then wrap the butter in it. While he'd prepare your butter, he might suggest that this week you should buy some of the new cheese, or he'd point out some reason why you might need more than your usual order, this week.

Once the butter was packed, you'd be given a slip of paper with the amount due on it and move to another part of the counter, perhaps to buy biscuits. If my brother and I were lucky, we might be given a few broken bits. Sometimes the assistant would persuade mother to buy a couple of the iced ones that we both liked. Biscuits were always served from large cube-shaped tins and be given to us loose in a paper bag. Anything bought was added to the note on the paper you were given.

When you were finished you'd go to the window at the large mahogany cash desk, at the back of the shop, which spanned the gap between the two counters. Here, under an impressive clock, reminiscent of something seen on railway station platforms, you paid for everything that you'd bought.

Depending on the site with which you do business, internet shopping can be much more like a visit to the old-style Sainsbury's than the modern supermarket. That's because most on-line stores will make suggestions about related items that you might want to buy and not just take your money for the item that you initially ordered, and they'll let you wander round their store, from department to department, picking things up as you go and not charge you until you have decided on your final purchase, though they will use the modern analogy of a supermarket check-out when you do decide that you have finished.

Browsing and Window Shopping

Whatever my claims about how some internet shopping may replicate the traditional High Street virtues of service, there are other aspects that do make it distinctly different. For example, if internet shopping is just mail order but from an on-line, rather than printed, catalogue then, you might ask, where is the opportunity to ask the sales assistant for more information about the product. Buying anything is rarely a matter of do you buy it or not, but more likely, should you buy this one or that. You frequently need help to make up your mind about which is the better buy for your needs.

Whilst there are some questions that only the assistant could answer, perhaps about whether they offer money-back guarantees, or promises to match another shop's prices, you know that they are in the game of maximising the sale and not necessarily in making sure you get the best product for you. You recognise that you might well get less biased and more knowledgeable answers to the questions that you have from an existing user of the goods, rather than a sales assistant. The Internet can help with that!

With all the variety of goods that are available these days and the rapid change in models of almost anything, it can be very difficult to find someone who has real experience with the item you are thinking of buying. Your circle of friends and acquaintances may not have the item you are thinking of buying. Your alternatives are to turn to magazine reviews, but unless you are buying something for an on-going hobby, you probably don't take the right magazine, or to visit the library to trawl through old copies of "Which", in the hope that the Consumers' Association has produced a recent report. What the Internet can do is put you in touch with just the users you need to provide you with the answers.

Web Site Reviews

Obviously the first thing to do is to see what information is available on web sites. Using the manufacturer's name and model number as the search terms, on a couple of different engines, will probably turn up a number of pages that are relevant.

To those not used to internet shopping the biggest surprise might be that many on-line stores have areas on their sites where buyers are invited to post comments on the products they sell. Not only do they allow feedback about the products but about the supplier as well. Some comments you can probably happily dismiss as not relevant, whilst others may provide worthwhile, real world experience.

You might think that the site owner would edit out bad reviews, but often adverse comments say as much about the poster as the product or supplier and the wise site owner lets all comments stand as posted. Indeed the only alternative is probably to withdraw the facility rather than try to massage it to show the company or its products in the best light. Think about it and you realise that deliberate censorship could easily generate such a flood of postings that the site owner would be sucked into such a workload that it would not be worthwhile to attempt to maintain it.

In any case, you frequently find that follow-up posts can often criticise or moderate earlier comments. For example, an early writer might comment on a design flaw in the item they had just bought. Another may add that wasn't a problem with theirs, and a more recent poster still reports that when they complained to the manufacturer they were immediately sent a replacement part that showed no fault.

Asking on Newsgroups

Another area of the Internet where one can find views on just about anything is newsgroups. Newsgroups allow an uncensored discussion of a huge range of topics. Because of their nature, newsgroups, like chat rooms, have a bad reputation, as it can be easy for children to gain access to unsuitable material. However, it is easy enough to avoid the less savoury aspects of the medium and it can prove very useful to the Internet shopper.

For occasional use, rather than use the conventional newsreader (See Appendix 2), it is easier simply to search at Google under the "Groups" tab. The process is identical to searching for web pages, except that the results shown are those for "articles", messages and comments, posted to the 50,000 plus topic areas that comprise the newsgroups. The articles are shown as being grouped into "threads", that is a cluster of postings, each one responding to an earlier posting under a single subject line. As with web page searching there is an "advanced groups search" that can be useful for separating out unwanted entries.

For the internet shopper the great advantage, the purpose even, of a newsgroup is that it is there to receive questions and comments, whereas web pages are largely static publications, which you are expected only to read, rather than contribute to. Google offers the ability to post both new articles and replies to existing posts, so it is quite easy to ask follow-up questions or to provide or ask for further details when necessary.

The one word of caution is that you should be sure that what you are posting is "on-topic" for your chosen group. Subscribers can sometimes get very upset by newcomers who do not follow the group's conventions. What is allowed is always recorded in a group's "charter". Many groups have a volunteer who maintains and posts a regular "FAQ" message for newcomers. It is a good idea to search through postings over the previous month to see if there is a post that includes "FAQ" in its subject line and read through it.

On most newsgroups you can expect to get responses to almost any message within a matter of hours, minutes in some cases.

Newsgroups can be especially useful to those who are on pay-as-you-go accounts as they are designed for off-line use when used with a newsreader. Post a question. Wait, off-line, for a an hour or so, then reconnect and pick up all the responses. It's just like picking up e-mail. There's no need to navigate to a particular web site to get the answers.

Those using newsreaders are able to "subscribe" to as many newsgroups as they like. There are no fees involved. Being subscribed just means that the software will start sending details of all the articles posted to that particular newsgroup. You then select the ones that you wish to read. For many, their hobby is to monitor a chosen selection of newsgroups that cover their hobbies or areas of expertise, and provide help to those who post questions there. Newsgroups are refreshingly empty of the commercial hard sell of many web sites. Being a text-based medium, newsgroups can also be useful to those with visual disabilities and use text to speech software.

Example - Buying more Memory

I had upgraded my computer to run the Windows XP operating system. This demands more processing power than my old operating system and leaves less room to run the programs that I use, so I had decided to increase the memory, RAM, in my system from 128k to 256k.

Find the Site

Magazine reviews had persuaded me to buy from Crucial Technology so, guessing, I entered the URL "www.crucial.co.uk" into the address bar of Internet Explorer. This did find me the Crucial web site. However, it automatically redirected me to "www.crucial.com". That was unfortunate. Everything was priced in dollars. Not what I was expecting! Contrary to what many will claim, at that time, after allowing for the exchange rate, the listed prices were not dramatically cheaper than UK prices. Not only that, if I had to pay any import duties, and not forgetting the extra delivery delay that I might expect when the package had to come from the US, the site did not appear to offer me the best deal.

A check in a magazine revealed my mistake. I needed to use:

http://www.crucial.com/uk

This reinforces the lesson learned earlier. There are a number of ways in which multi-national companies might support local regions. Crucial use what is probably the second most popular after "companyname.co.uk".

Terms and Conditions

If you've not used a site before then you might want reassurance that this is a company that you want to trust. The first thing to check, if you can, is the terms and conditions that the site imposes. The best sites will allow you to check these before going to the "check-out". Unfortunately, many sites do not give you a chance to read them until you are about to finally confirm your order.

In particular, you'll want to know what happens about goods that need returning because of a fault, delay in delivery, or unsuitability for your purpose. Use the same kind of judgements as you would for any other shop.

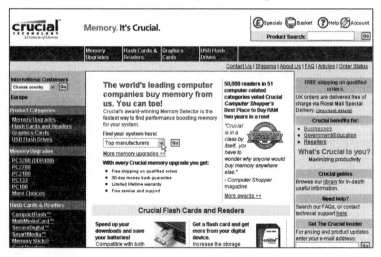

General Support

As with any shop, another thing to look for is evidence that the company does more than sell the product and can provide appropriate background information about the items it sells. In this case I am buying a technical product and fitting it to my computer requires that I open the case and get inside. In cases like this you'll be reassured if the site provides guides for doing this kind of work. The site I have chosen meets these requirements with prominent links to fitting guides and pages of answers to FAQs, Frequently Asked Questions.

Select the Product

Once satisfied that it is a company that I am happy to buy from, it's time to look for the product I need. The "Find your system here" box allows me to search for my computer manufacturer and model.

After a couple of screens the details are revealed. I am offered the choice of two products to fit my machine. I only need one, so do not need to change the default quantity, and click the "Buy" button, but not before I have checked the other links on the page that confirm that there are no special factors which I need to take account of with my particular model of computer.

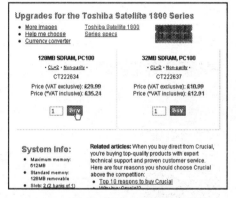

When the buy button is clicked, I am moved to a screen that indicates my current bill. At some sites this would be known as the "shopping basket" screen. It shows both VAT and shipping charges, indicating the total that I will be charged. As is typical, details of further products in which I might be interested are also shown on this screen. However, I only want the one product and ignore the invitation to consider these. I click the "Checkout" link.

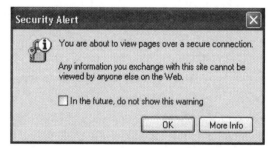

crucial
TECHNOLOGY
A Division of Micron

Memory. **It's Crucial.**

Update	Qty.	Part Number	Description	Price (ea.) VAT exclusive	Total
Update	1	CT222834	128MB, 144-pin SODIMM Upgrade for a Toshiba Satellite 1800 Series System	£29.99	£29.99
				Basket Total:	£29.99
				Shipping Charge:	£—
		Coupon savings! If you have a coupon code, you can enter it later in the checkout process.		VAT calculated at 17.5% for United Kingdom:	£5.25
				Sub total:	£35.24

< Continue Shopping   Checkout >

Other Great Products

128MB CompactFlash™
£26.99
(VAT exclusive)
£31.71
(*VAT inclusive)
Buy

64MB MultiMediaCard™
£21.99
(VAT exclusive)
£25.84
(*VAT inclusive)
Buy

All prices shown in UK pounds excluding any applicable delivery charges. * - VAT calculated at 17.5% for United Kingdom.

The Crucial "shopping basket" screen shows the items that you have decided to buy and suggests further purchases

The Checkout Process

Before moving to the Checkout page a dialogue box appears. If this had not appeared I would have aborted my sale at this point and sought an alternative site for my custom.

Security Alert ☒

(i) You are about to view pages over a secure connection.

Any information you exchange with this site cannot be viewed by anyone else on the Web.

☐ In the future, do not show this warning

OK   More Info

This dialogue reveals the vital information that I am about to view pages over a secure connection, with the explanation that, this means that from now until I leave the secure connection, any information flowing between my computer and the site cannot be read by anyone else on the web. It is this facility that gives me the confidence to enter my credit card details and send them over the net.   With a secure connection I can be sure that only those necessary to complete the transaction can have access to the information.

The dialogue includes a check box that allows you to avoid seeing this intrusive dialogue again.   If you do that then in future the only indication that you get that you are connected to a secure server is the small padlock symbol on the status line of the browser.   Personally, I prefer the reassurance of the large warning dialogue, and a similar one to tell me I have left that connection, to a small icon on the status line of the browser.

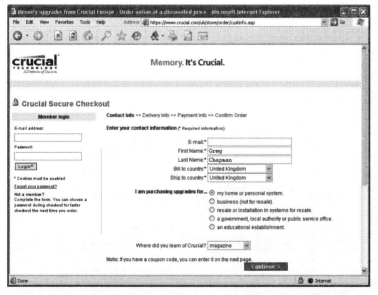

The first of the Crucial Checkout screens, showing the padlock symbol on the status line of the browser

The top of this Checkout page indicates that there are four parts to the process and that this is the first, designed to collect the "Contact Info". Many sites will ask for all the information, contact, delivery and payment on a single page before moving to the order confirmation page.

After completing the boxes for e-mail address, name and shipping and billing countries, and answering various other customer survey information, I click the Continue button, which takes me to the next, "Delivery Info" page.

Here it is a simple matter of entering the address details onto the screen. As is usual, a number of the boxes are marked as "required". If you failed to complete some of these essential boxes you would find the page would be rejected. You'd be returned to this same page with notes about the errors and invited to re-submit a corrected page. Again, at Crucial, the details of your complete order are added, for your information at the bottom of the page.

The Crucial site contains the reminder on this page to users of credit cards that deliveries to addresses other than the card holders are not normally allowed, unless the credit card company has been previously informed. If you are likely to be at work, or out for some other reason, when a delivery is attempted, then specifying a different address, such as a neighbour's, is obviously useful. Do make such arrangements in advance of placing such an order.

The third stage in the checkout process is to select your payment method and provide the necessary details. This part should be straightforward. Lower on the page is an invitation to provide a password for use with your e-mail address as an identification method when tracking the progress of your order. This password need not be the same, some would argue should not be the same, as that which you use to log onto your account at your ISP. This password will only be used in connection with your "account" at Crucial. You are also asked to pick a security question from a list.

This is used, as a slightly less secure way, to confirm your identity should you forget your password.

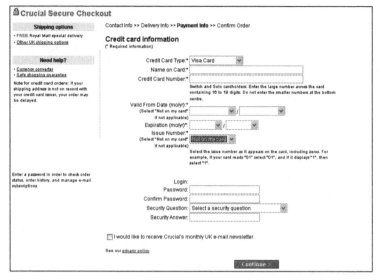

The final "Confirm Order" page reprints all the essential information, and gives you a chance to check and amend it. Here I have blanked out the personal details:

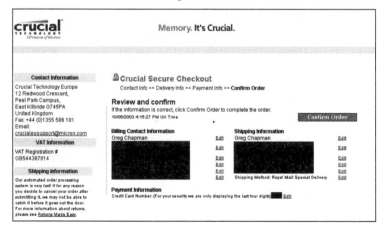

As before, below this is a repeat of the order details. This time there is also a summary of the terms and conditions of trading, with a link to the full terms provided. It only remains to click the "Confirm Order" button. Once this is done a similar screen appears, but this new version contains an "Order Request Number" and confirms that an e-mail has been sent to the address given on the first of the Checkout screens, confirming all the order details.

In my case the order was placed at 4:18pm on a Tuesday afternoon and the goods arrived in the post early on Thursday morning. A note elsewhere on the Crucial site told me that had I placed the order before midday then I should have expected the goods to have arrived on the Wednesday morning.

Had my goods not arrived when expected, I could have re-visited the Crucial site and followed the "Order status" link. I would have needed to log on using the e-mail address and password I entered when placing the order and once logged on could have examined the state of the outstanding order, checking where in the system it was. It would, at least, have told me whether or when the order had been despatched or where in the carrier's system it might be. That would have given me the chance of approaching the right people, had there been any cause for complaint.

This was a good example of the benefits of mail order at its best. Living in the heart of rural Norfolk I do not have easy access to large specialist computer stores, with a full range in stock of components to fit a particular model of computer. By buying on-line, I was able to select and have the right components delivered with the minimum of fuss or delay.

Example - Buying a Camera

I had decided to replace my first digital camera and was waiting for the prices to fall to where the specification that I wanted was available for around £200. I was browsing in a local store and found one that seemed to have a specification well above my target level and claimed to be much reduced in price, but still £65 above my budget. But, as ever, with these kinds of goods, it was impossible to find anyone in the store who could answer my more technical questions or tell me much more than was printed on the box. Once back home I was surprised to find the same model in the Argos catalogue priced at £350, so my local store appeared to be offering a bargain. But I didn't want to buy it without further research, so it was time to turn to the Internet.

Searching for Information

Using the manufacturer's name and model number as the search terms, on a couple of different engines, turned up a number of pages that suggested there would be information about this camera. However, looking at a number of these pages, I could find no references to the camera I wanted. This was no surprise!

Digital cameras along with most consumer electronics these days have a very short model life, often measured in weeks rather than months. What had happened was that the search engines had last indexed the pages they were listing a few weeks before, and the pages had since been updated and no longer contained the text indicated in the search engine's files.

In spite of this problem, I still managed to find a number of sites with relevant information and a number with the particular model for sale and I spent a few minutes selecting, copying and pasting large chunks of text from these postings into Notepad to examine later when off-line.

Some of the sites I found invited those posting comments to give a brief description of themselves and their qualifications for making their review. This helped distinguish between those who claimed to be a "first time buyer", a "keen photographer", or a "professional". Obviously, there is no vetting of these descriptions, but they were good indicators of the kind of comments that might be made in the entry.

The postings I found provided some very helpful insights about the camera in which I was interested. One writer said that the design of the lens cap was flawed and easily dropped off the camera. A later poster said that, that wasn't a problem with their camera, and another said that when they complained to the manufacturer they were immediately sent a replacement lens cap that showed no fault.

One of the things I was worried about was the electronic viewfinder, which I was afraid would consume battery power. I found reassurance on this, but a warning that it could be inadequate in low lighting conditions. Some comments I could dismiss, as I knew that they lacked some understanding about the product. Others were obviously from those who had experience of a range of cameras, whose comments I valued more highly. On balance I decided that this was the camera for me.

Further comments revealed that it was an obsolete model, but its replacement used the same chassis and lens. This accounted for the fact that my local Argos had none in stock and why it hadn't been reduced in its recent sale. The new model, though much cheaper than the old one at its original list price, lacked some of its features and remained more expensive than the price that the last few of the obsolete model were now fetching. The going rate, it seemed, was not £265 but under £230, and given the better specification than I had planned, this was close enough to my budget to be worth the extra. Without the Internet I would not have been able to find this out and make these judgements.

The Purchase

I elected to buy the camera from Amazon. It was not quite the cheapest place offering the camera I had selected, but I had done business with Amazon before and was satisfied with their service. Perhaps because it was one of the most highly discounted cameras on offer at the site, it was the featured item on the "Electronics & Photo" page.

My selected camera was the featured photographic product, so it was just a matter of clicking "Add to Shopping Basket"

The Amazon site can be confusing when first encountered. Partly, this is because they offer goods at a number of prices.

Apart from an "Our Price" figure, on my visit they were offering cheaper "Used and New" prices. In this case the panel "More Buying Choices" reveals that they were also offering a refurbished model as well as people wishing to sell their own second-hand cameras. I had decided to buy new from them and noted that they were down to their last three in stock.

Selecting Extras

In keeping with the normal habit of major on-line retailers, after selecting my main purchase, I am offered a number of optional extras, in two lists. The first are obvious accessories and the second, a list of purchases that others who have bought the product have chosen to buy at the same time.

**Here I am about to add a memory card to the items in the
"Your Shopping Basket" panel. This already shows the
camera and also keeps a running total of my purchases**

I had found a need to expand the memory card in my earlier camera, so I decided to buy the largest of the memory cards on offer. Many of the reviews I had read also recommended this. The page changes once again and shows an updated shopping basket, with the most recent selection illustrated, and a further selection of possible purchases. These include mains adaptors, battery chargers, memory card readers and various cases for the camera.

You need to be careful in making some of these selections. For example, I wanted a case to go with the camera, but by the time I'd got to this stage in the purchase I was being offered items, including cases, that did not relate to my camera, but instead to things that others had bought when buying the same memory card. When I clicked the "Proceed to Checkout" link, I was to realise that I had initially picked an inappropriate case.

It turned out that selecting the right case would have been impossible if all I had to go on were the descriptions provided by Amazon. There was no case offered which matched the model number of my selected camera. However, newsgroup postings that I had retrieved using the "Groups" search facility at Google had revealed that in the United States the equivalent model had a totally different model number and there was a case available on Amazon described as fitting that model. However, that particular item was not illustrated and I was keen to have a case that was as small as possible and with pockets to take spare sets of batteries and similar essential extras. I had no way of telling if the one that was available would suit my needs.

Having got a wrong item in the shopping basket, I needed to click the "Edit Shopping Basket" link. This took me to a screen where I could remove items or adjust quantities. Once the change had been made, once more I clicked the "Proceed to Checkout" link.

The Checkout

The initial Amazon checkout page suggests that there is a complex seven-step process, from Welcome to Confirm, needed to complete the purchase. However, it depends on some of your choices on whether all of these are needed.

As a returning customer on the Checkout Welcome screen I enter the e-mail address I used previously and the password I set up on my first "new customer" visit

The Welcome screen includes the statement "If you received an error message when you tried to use our secure server, sign in using our standard server". Doing this is not to be recommended! It's there simply so you are not tempted to lose Amazon its sale. As the page explains, if you select a secure server all traffic to and from that page is encrypted, so stopping unauthorised people from being able to read that information. Accepting use of the standard server is the Internet equivalent of handing your credit card to a stranger and allowing it to be passed on to anyone else to make the payment for you. Of course, many people do this kind of thing in restaurants and don't worry about it, so you shouldn't be any more fearful of it on the Internet.

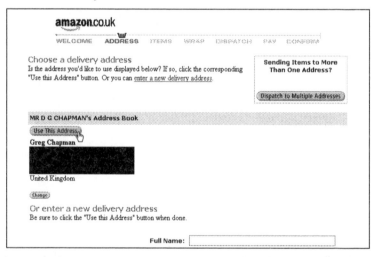

As a previous customer, my address is "on file", but there are options to change it or use a different address for this order

Step two allows entry of a delivery address. Existing customers can pick from addresses previously used. I want the goods to be delivered to the address that my last order was sent to, so I can click the "Use This Address" button above my home address. In my case it moves me to the "Pay" screen, but for those sending to an address that is not that held by the credit card issuer there will be some additional steps, as there will for those electing to have Amazon gift-wrap your purchases.

Details of previous payment methods are kept, but you may opt to choose an alternative method for this purchase

As with the previous screens, the Pay screen assumes that you will use a payment method used previously, but allows the shopper to select an alternative method. In my case, my previously used card has now expired and I need to enter details of a new card. It would also be possible to pay by cheque. If you take this option, you are taken to a screen that describes how long the goods will be held for whilst awaiting for the cheque to arrive and be cleared.

Having completed the payment method screen you reach the final "Confirm" page. This is the most important in any transaction. It is the last chance you have to alter any of the contract details. The main part of the screen confirms the goods ordered, delivery address, delivery method and costs.

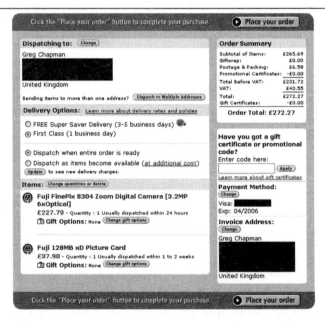

The main panel on the order confirmation screen.
Always read the "small print" shown on the rest of the page

At Amazon there is no simple way to know what the delivery charges will be until reaching this final confirmation screen. By default, Amazon will dispatch your goods by the quickest, and most expensive, method. So the first thing to check is that this charge is acceptable. Amazon, as with a number of other internet shops, offers free delivery, subject to certain conditions. In essence these are that you need to wait until the entire order is ready and you accept the slower three to five business days for processing.

In my case, the summary of my order stated that one of the items I was ordering would take one to two weeks, but the other could be dispatched within 24 hours. I wanted the camera within a week, but was happy to wait till later for the additional memory card. I decided that it would be better not to place the order for both items at once, so I deleted the memory card from my order. Once I had returned to the order confirmation screen the section on the left, for selecting whether items should be dispatched individually or only when the whole order was ready, had disappeared. Now I could opt for the camera to be sent by the "FREE Super Saver Delivery" method at no shipping cost.

I confirmed the order by clicking the "Place your order" button and was greeted with a message that said an e-mail was being sent that confirmed the details. This indeed arrived within moments, timed at 16:19 on a Friday afternoon. It told me that dispatch was expected on the following Tuesday, with delivery by the following day or the day after that. A second e-mail was sent at 06:53 on the Tuesday morning confirming that my goods had been despatched, sent by a named courier service. This arrived at my ISP at 7:08 and the goods arrived at about 8:20am on the Wednesday morning. The young woman apologised for being so early, saying that she found that Amazon customers often seemed to be out if she called later, so she tried to deliver those parcels first.

Summary

This chapter compared traditional high-street shopping, catalogue shopping and internet shopping and concluded that the Internet can provide the benefits of both the other two forms of shopping. The internet shop often has the best price, a level of service not found in many conventional shops these days and the opportunity to obtain opinions of real users of the goods rather than only that of a salesman.

Outside of the "shop", on the Internet you can also gather views of things you are thinking of buying from a much wider circle than just friends and acquaintances.

Two example purchases were followed through. One purchase was a first-time visit to a single product (computer memory) business that was not set up to encourage return visits or additional purchases. The second was a return visit, to buy a camera, to a business that does all it can to encourage repeat purchases. It does this by such things as offering further suggestions with each item selected for purchase, and by offering to buy back goods so it can offer them on second-hand.

The actual purchases involved picking goods and visiting a "checkout", which involved supplying credit card information, when it was not already held on record, and making decisions about delivery options.

Other matters mentioned, or alluded to, included:

- The need to record usernames and passwords, to avoid having to re-supply personal information when re-visiting a site

- The need to double-check all purchase details, particularly dates, sizes, colours, part numbers and so forth

- The importance of only using a secure server when posting credit card details to a web site

- The need to be aware of delivery and, particularly when buying from abroad, other charges

- The importance of keeping all necessary records in case a query arises with the order.

12 The Buying Process

13

Worries

Buying On-Line

So far this book has explained what you need and how to connect to the Internet, how to use the software that you'll need, once connected, and how to find the sites where you can buy the goods and services you want. Finally, it worked through, screen-by-screen, a couple of purchases made on-line. Now you should feel ready to make your first purchase, but it would only be natural to have a few worries about that first purchase.

Broadly, such worries will fall into two groups, some about the whole business of "distance shopping" and others about technical issues to do with the computer and the Internet connection that you will be using. Each will be examined in turn. Distance shopping is the term used by some to describe any purchases not made "over the counter" in a shop. The first chapter of this book said that buying on-line is really nothing more than mail order, and whether the purchase is made by post, through a telephone call or on-line, the issues will be the same whatever the form of "distance shopping" employed.

Site Worries

Before Buying

Before you buy something at a conventional shop you'll decide whether you can trust it. Mostly, you don't think twice about shops in the High Street. The company will have invested a lot in the site and building and has a name to protect. It is not likely to squander it on poor service. The same may not be true of the back-street shop or market stall. Such places tend to come and go and may not provide the back-up of a large nationally known business.

When you first visit a web site you might be impressed with its general appearance, but it costs little to build an impressive site and it is impossible to judge a site on appearance alone.

Is it Based in the UK?

If you are thinking about buying from a company that you are not familiar with then be cautious. Just because there is a "uk" in the URL does not mean that it is UK-based. Always check that you can contact the business by means other than the web and e-mail alone. Look for a real world address, phone and fax numbers. If the address is UK based you can use business finder web sites to see if you can locate them (See Appendix 1 – "Find things in the Real World").

Do you Want to Buy from Overseas?

You will hear many people say that they managed to buy much cheaper abroad. That may be true, but be aware of some of the potential problems.

If you are buying electrical goods, for example, will the goods be supplied with the right voltages? Will it be possible to fit the correct plug? Some items, notably DVDs, are designed to work only in equipment sold for use in a particular country.

Are the guarantees that are offered valid when the goods are used overseas? If there is a claim under a guarantee, will the costs of returning the goods for repair or replacement make it viable?

Have you taken account of any taxes and duties that will become liable as the goods enter the country? I am particularly sensitive to this after the American agent of a Swiss software house sent me a Christmas present. I had become an unpaid volunteer tester of one of the company's products. Out of the blue I received a card from the Post Office telling me that there was a package to collect which required payment before delivery. It turned out to be a CD-ROM containing software in which I had no interest. The agent had indicated on the customs declaration that it had a value of £250. I had to pay duty, before I was allowed to open it to see that it was of no use to me!

If things do go really badly wrong and the purchase was of a significant size then bear in mind that suing a supplier based overseas can be difficult, expensive and take a lot of time. The terms and conditions of supply may indicate that the contract may be governed by the laws of the country from where the goods were supplied rather than bought, or even by some other country. The web site of the Office of Fair Trading has some useful pointers on these issues and is worth looking at before committing yourself to a large overseas purchase.

Will your Data be Shared?

Look on the site for a "privacy statement". This should tell you what they do with the information they have about you. Some may say that they reserve the right to forward it to companies offering related services or products. UK and EU based companies should provide an option for you to bar them from doing this. Beyond the EU there may be no such restrictions.

What about "The Small Print"?

It is also important to look for the terms and conditions of supply. Check whether the packing and shipping charges are included in the cheap-looking "headline" prices. Are there indications of whether all goods advertised are in stock, or when despatch and delivery should be expected. How should goods be returned? Some of the major UK high-street shops allow goods bought from their web sites to be returned to a local store, others will send a van to collect unsuitable goods. If these options are not allowed, then you may be left with an expensive bill to return unwanted goods.

Trust Schemes

The Kite Mark; CORGI Registered Gas Installer; Member of the Federation of Master Builders, Woolsafe Approved Certified Operator. A quick glance through Yellow Pages reveals a host of registration and approval schemes for all kinds of trades and businesses. A couple of years ago there were a host of schemes about that aimed to provide the same kind of reassurance for internet traders.

As the Internet has matured these schemes are disappearing. For example, there used to be a scheme backed by the Institute of Chartered Accountants and another by the Consumers Association. Both are gone. The cynic might claim that this shows that there is no one to be trusted. The contrary view is that it indicates that the fears that were once prevalent in buyers have largely disappeared and traders no longer feel the need to demonstrate their honesty and efficiency.

If you still seek reassurance then look for the "TrustUK" logo. The UK government endorses the scheme, which, early in 2004, was unfortunately in a state of flux, following the closure of the "Which? Web Trader" scheme.

Find out about the TrustUK scheme at their web site at http://www.trustuk.org.uk

Companies displaying the logo are members of trade associations or subscriber bodies that operate codes of practice to which their members are required to adhere. TrustUK approves these bodies. Approval should assure that these companies will:

- Protect your privacy

- Ensure that your payments are secure

- Help you to make an informed buying decision

- Let you know what you have agreed to - and how to cancel orders should you need to

- Deliver the goods or services ordered within the agreed time period

- Protect children

- Sort out any complaints, wherever you live

While Buying

Always be suspicious of businesses that ask you for any more information than is required to deliver the goods and charge for them. As mentioned already make sure that the site has switched you to a "secure server" when asking you for details of your credit card. This is sometimes described as moving to a "Secure Socket Layer" and is usually indicated by the closed padlock symbol on the status line of the browser.

Use a Credit Card

If possible, pay by credit card when the goods or services cost more than £100 for an item (but less than £30,000). It may give some extra protection compared with payment by debit or charge card. This is because if you have a claim against the seller you may also have a claim against your credit card issuer and this can be useful if the seller goes out of business.

Keep Records

You should always keep a record of your purchase details in case of problems with the order or the goods when delivered. Reputable businesses will send an e-mail to confirm the order as the order is completed. However, if you have concerns about your computer or the stability of your Internet connection then it maybe worthwhile saving the web pages with the necessary information on them as the checkout process is being completed. That way, in the event of the non-arrival of the confirming e-mail you still have detailed information about the order. Ways to do this were explained in Chapter Seven.

After Buying

Having placed the order, you should expect an e-mail confirming the order to arrive within a few minutes. When it does, providing it contains all the necessary information, you should feel able to delete any screen dumps that you took.

If delivery was not promised immediately from stock, you should expect further e-mails to report the progress of your order, especially if the company expects a delay beyond that initially indicated. Any e-mails that do appear should offer you the opportunity to cancel the order, or accept alternative goods. Finally an e-mail should arrive confirming that your goods have been despatched and the goods should arrive.

When Complaining

If the worst does happen and the goods are faulty, not as ordered or do not arrive at all, you are reduced to the same procedure that you would have used with conventional mail order. The terms and conditions should have indicated the appropriate procedure, and possibly you have other rights under the terms of any trust schemes that formed part of the benefits of shopping with the company concerned.

In general, you need to contact the company initially. Your e-mail should mention: the date of any advert or website where the goods appeared, the date of the order; the details of the goods or service ordered; the amount paid and method of payment, any reference (e.g. order or customer reference number), the reason for the complaint, anything else relevant and how you would like your claim resolved. In addition mention any rights that apply in the event of one of the trust schemes having been part of the conditions.

Technical Worries

Apart from the worries you may have about mail order in general, the other likely area of concern is the technical side of the purchase, or simply being on-line. This could come in two areas, your own computer or the problems with the site from which you are making a purchase.

Your Computer

The Need for a Firewall

You may have read stories of hackers reading, downloading, or deleting someone else's files, or installing programs on another's computer and running them under remote control. It is possible for this to happen without any obvious signs to the owner of the computer under attack.

Firewalls, when properly configured, can remove this threat. Dial-up users will normally run a software firewall. Broadband users may find one is built into the hardware of their router or modem.

A firewall is not normally considered necessary for those on a dial-up connection unless they expect to stay on-line for long periods. This is because most dial-up connections present a different address to any potential hacker each time they connect and it is unlikely that a hacker will have time to discover any opening and do any damage. If you have a broadband connection and expect to stay on-line for long periods then most people will tell you that it is foolish not to have a firewall. However, in spite of being sold as "always on", it is quite possible to end an Internet session, and come off-line.

Even on broadband you are only likely to be more vulnerable than those with an ordinary telephone line connection if you are running programs that actively allow others access to your machine, such as web or FTP server programs or you allow telnet access to your machine. For readers of this book, who are likely to be coming to the Internet for the first time and only considering doing a little shopping and banking, these are not the programs that are likely to be used.

In fact, Windows XP includes a simple firewall program. This will prevent unexpected inbound traffic from reaching your computer. As it is bundled with the operating system, then one might as well always have it enabled.

Put simply, those at whom this book is aimed should not be unduly worried about these issues; however, it is always prudent to install anti-virus software.

The Virus Menace

Viruses are programs, often sent unintentionally by others as attachments to e-mails. It is possible for such programs, once running on your computer to completely destroy all data on the hard disc. However, many that are in circulation these days seem to be primarily aimed at disrupting Microsoft's web site and damaging the software giant's market credibility. That is not to say that individuals can ignore the threat. One of the most disruptive viruses in circulation in 2003 would disable an individual's computer from connecting to the Internet, or disconnect it and shut it down, losing the user any unsaved work. A number of software houses providing anti-virus software can be found in Appendix 1.

A Computer Crash

Most people have, at some time, experienced their computer locking up. The keyboard may refuse to respond. The mouse may not move the pointer. The screen may appear corrupted or nothing happens when an object is clicked. This is known as a "crash". One or more of the programs running on the computer has done something unexpected by the programmer and has run wild with the computer's memory, stopping it from working. If the keyboard is still responding, the usual advice is to hold down the Control and Alt keys and tap Delete. This should bring up a "Task Manager" window, which should allow you to shut down any of the programs that are listed as "not responding". If the computer does not respond to this keystroke, then it may be that the only thing that can be done is to pull the plug from the wall.

If this does happen while you are part way through an on-line purchase, then it should just be a matter of re-starting the computer, reconnecting to the Internet and the site, and starting all over again. If this happens as you click the button to commit to the purchase, then if there is an e-mail awaiting you when you reconnect to the Internet, there has been no problem. If none arrives then you can assume that the purchase did not proceed and you will have to restart the purchase.

Although all these things are possible, they are highly unlikely to happen unless you have a large number of windows open and are attempting to do other tasks whilst on-line shopping.

The Site

It is also possible for a web site to become overloaded and for it to crash. When the government first put the data from the 1901 census on-line, it proved so popular that it crashed. Demand was also unexpectedly high when the Inland Revenue first made on-line completion of Tax Returns available.

This possibility should not be a worry with a normal shopping site. A site is likely to become intolerably slow and unresponsive long before you reach the checkout stage and are committing to a purchase. In the same way that you might abandon queuing in a Post Office because the wait will be too long, you will give up on a site that is becoming overloaded and wait until you can return at a little less busy time.

If the site does go down at the moment when you should receive confirmation that the order has been accepted and an e-mail has been sent to confirm this, then if you don't receive that e-mail, you can be fairly sure that the order was not accepted. The best course of action would, initially, be to e-mail the business with as much information about the transaction, especially the precise date and time and ask if their records show that a purchase order was accepted. If the site appears more permanently off-line then it's time to turn to those alternative methods of contacting the company that you checked out earlier in the buying process.

Summary

This was a chapter of two parts. The first was a list of sensible precautions, so your experience of on-line banking and shopping is more pleasant, should something go wrong. The second was a list of solutions to technical issues that might arise. Importantly, none of the tales of possible doom outlined in this chapter should put you off Internet banking and shopping.

These matters needed to be covered only for the sake of completeness. It's possible I might get run over by a bus today, but fear of that possibility does not stop me from going out, any more than fear of the Internet should put you off having a go at Internet banking and shopping! To paraphrase the closing words to every Crime Watch broadcast, "Don't have nightmares. Everything described here really is very rare."

The benefit of becoming a confident on-line banker and shopper, especially for those of the older generation, is immense. Carefully built-up savings can be made to go further, by leaving the money in the most beneficial accounts for longer. Shopping around for the best prices is no longer an exhausting slog from shop to shop. For those of us who don't live near the great shopping centres, finding those little aids to daily life can be difficult, but to an internet shopper, they are no further away than our computer. There's never a heavy bag to carry when all your shopping is delivered straight to your door. That alone is a joy, especially as one finds it more difficult to get about and get a parking space or bus stop near to the shop we need!

Isn't it time you were on-line?

Appendix 1

Suggested Sites

Before you get On-Line:

Sites that include reviews of ISPs:

>http://www.ispreview.co.uk
>http://www.adslguide.org.uk
>http://www.net4nowt.com

Sites for On-Line Shopping Guidance:

>http://www.oft.gov.uk/Consumer
>http://www.tradingstandards.gov.uk
>http://www.adviceguide.org.uk

Trader Approval Scheme:

>http://www.trustuk.org.uk

Search Tools:

>http://www.alltheweb.com/
>http://www.altavista.com/web/text
>http://www.ask.co.uk/
>http://www.bbc.co.uk
>http://www.bbc.co.uk/cgi-bin/
>education/betsie/parser.pl
>http://google.co.uk
>http://s.teoma.com/AdvancedSearch
>http://www.yahoo.co.uk

Search Guidance:

http://www.searchenginewatch.com

Shops, Stores and Supermarkets:

High Street:

http://www.argos.co.uk
http://www.asda.co.uk
http://www.boots.com
http://www.debenhams.com
http://www.harrods.com
http://www.johnlewis.com
http://www.lauraashley.com
http://www.marksandspencer.com
http://www.sainsburystoyou.com
http://www.tesco.com
http://www.whsmith.co.uk
http://www.woolworths.co.uk

On-Line:

http://www.amazon.co.uk
http://www.ebay.co.uk
http://www.lastminute.com
http://www.preloved.co.uk

Shopping Portals:

http://www.dealtime.co.uk
http://www.shopperuk.com

Over 50s Portals

(with lots of Banking and Shopping Links):

http://www.50connect.co.uk
http://www.cennet.co.uk

http://www.laterlife.com
http://www.seniority.co.uk
http://www.silversurfers.net

Banks and Building Societies:

http://www.alliance-leicester.co.uk
http://www.barclays.com
http://www.halifax.co.uk
http://www.hsbc.com
http://www.lloydstsb.com
http://www.nationwide.co.uk
http://www.natwest.com

Miscellaneous:

Find things in the real world:

http://www.bt.com/directory-enquiries
http://www.multimap.com
http://www.thomsonlocal.com
http://www.upmystreet.com
http://www.yell.com

Anti-Virus Software:

http://symantec.com
http://uk.mcafee.com
http://www.sophos.com
http://www.grisoft.com

General Interest:

http://www.over50.gov.uk

1 Appendix

Appendix 2

Other Internet Services

E-Mail and the (World Wide) Web are just two of the services available on the Internet, and the ones used for banking and shopping, so this book has concentrated on them. However, there are other services that your ISP will provide. This appendix provides a brief introduction to the other facilities that may be available to you.

Usenet/Newsgroups

Usenet, a corruption of "Users Network", provides a huge range of newsgroups, and is, perhaps, the next most significant service. In spite of the name "newsgroups", they have little to do with news. Instead, Usenet can be thought of as another form of e-mail. The difference is that instead of writing to a known individual or organisation, perhaps with a number of copies sent to a handful of others, when you post to a newsgroup you are, effectively, posting it on a public notice board. Anyone who wants to read the messages, known as articles, posted on that particular notice board will be sent a copy. As a poster, you cannot tell who will read it, it could be many thousands of people, or very few.

Most ISPs offer between 30,000 and 50,000 newsgroups each dedicated to a different topic. Some will have thousands of articles posted each day. Others barely manage a handful in a month. To avoid being swamped with newsgroup traffic the program that is used to collect them, known as a newsreader, is normally set to download the "headers" of each article. This is known as "subscribing" to a newsgroup and use of this term is probably what puts many people off finding out more. Don't be confused. It does not mean money needs to change hands. Usenet is a free service.

The headers reveal only the date, time, poster's name and subject line of the article. On seeing these, the user of the newsreader then marks those articles which he wishes to download and read in full. Usenet is especially useful to those on pay-as-you-go connections, as unlike the web, you do not have to be on-line while you read the articles.

Normally, for dial-up account holders, using Usenet will be a three-stage process. Connect for a few moments while you download the latest batch of headers for the groups to which you are subscribed. Once off-line, scan the headers and mark any that you wish to read in full, then re-connect to download the desired article bodies. Of course, in the normal course of events, each time you connect you will download more new headers. While you are connected you may also send your responses to articles that you have previously downloaded, or you may post new articles of your own. So, in reality, the three steps all run into each other in a cyclical process, as it will for broadband users.

Most ISPs expect their customers to use Outlook Express as their newsreader. This comes bundled with Windows and is the program normally used for e-mail, so there is almost nothing new to learn. If you have problems with something, or are an expert, or just have an interest in a topic, then there is probably a newsgroup that is just right for you.

Mail Lists

Mail Lists are similar to newsgroups, except that the ordinary
e-mail system is used to transport the messages and they do
not need your ISP to provide a "news server". These days it
is easiest to find a mail list from one of the web sites
dedicated to hosting them, such as www.yahoogroups.com or
www.topica.com.

Where newsgroups are a free service, mail lists operated
from commercial web sites like these are paid for by
advertisements appended to every message. However, unlike
newsgroups, they are very easy for anyone to set up. They
don't have to be large-scale public affairs. It is quite possible
to start a private mail list through these sites, as a way of
passing news and gossip around family members.

If a mail list gets very busy then you can find your e-mail
inbox swamped with traffic and difficult to manage. One
option is to visit the host's web site, turn off the direct
delivery of the mail and read the messages through the site
instead. Another possible benefit is that a mail list is
managed by its "owner" and so is policed in a way that a
newsgroup is not.

Chat Rooms

Chat Rooms are similar to newsgroups, except that instead of
posting messages for others to pick up and read later,
everything is done "live". Chat Rooms, therefore, are not for
pay-as-you-go customers! On entering a chat room, your
presence is notified to those already there. Anything that you
type is echoed immediately to anyone else in the "room", and
they will be able to respond immediately. The "chat" is all
typed, so much "shorthand" is used, and this can make it

confusing to newcomers, not used to the jargon. Some describe it as more like a CB radio conversation. Chat Rooms get a very bad press, because of paedophilia issues, but have been extremely useful in the past for the dissemination of serious news events. Much of the eyewitness information about the cruise missile attacks on Baghdad in the first Gulf War reached the west from chat rooms, the same happened earlier, during the storming of the Moscow White House, when Boris Yeltsin came to power.

Other Services

There are further services available, most of which have been available from the earliest days of the Internet, before it became available as a public medium. Most of these are of a somewhat technical nature and not designed for the casual user. The one exception is FTP, File Transfer Protocol. FTP is the way usually used to get a web site that you might create uploaded, and placed on-line, for others to be able to visit. However, you've got the wrong book, if you want to learn about that.

Index

A

Accessibility Options
  Setting   81
Address
  See URL
Advanced Search
  See Searching
AltaVista
  Advanced Search Help
       143

B

Banking
  Account Details   157
  Account Management
      167
  Introduced   11
  Logging on   155
  On-Line   154
  On-Line Applications
      168
  Payments   165
  Statement Download
      161
  Statements   160
  Transfers   163
Broadband
  Described   6, 29

Browser   3
  Address Bar   56
  Back & Fwd Buttons 70
  Customising   79
  Favorites   72
  History   71
  Launching   63
  Links Bar   60, 75
  Menu Bar   55
  Status Line   61
  Tool Bar   56
  Tour   55
  Working with   62
Buying
  Camera Example   186
  Data   17
  Goods   14
  Memory Example   177
  Music   18
  Services   16
  Terms and Conditions
      178
  Where to   19

C

Colours
  Setting   83

Index

Computer
    Public Access   23
    Suitable   26
Connecting
    Requirements   23
Connection
    Choice   27
Costs
    of connection   35
CSV   161
Cyber Cafés   24

D

Data
    Buying   17
Dial Up
    Described   28
Directories
    See Web Directories

E

E-Mail
    Settings   51
Excel   162

F

Favorites   72
Fonts
    Setting   83
Frames
    Described   96

H

History
    Setting Period   81

Home Page
    Browser   58
    Setting   79
    Web Site   58
http://   106
Hyperlinks
    Defined   4
    Using   65

I

Internet
    Defined   2
Internet Explorer
    See Browser
Internet Referral Service
                           44
Internet Service Provider
    CD-ROM   43
    Choice   27
    Defined   6
    Manual Set Up   48
    Opening Account   39
Internet shopping
    Why   6
ISP
    See Internet Service
    Provider

L

Library
    Computers   24
Link
    Selecting   4
Lotus 123   162

M

Modem
Broadband 33
Described 5
External 31
Internal 32
Type 30

N

Newsgroups 175
Charter 176

P

Password
Selecting 41
Printing
Background Colours 100
Dialogue Options Tab
98
Frames 96
Header and Footer
Codes 93
Print Dialogue 94
Screen Dumps 101
Product Reviews 174, 175

R

Records
Keeping 89

S

Screen Dumps
See Printing

Screen Space
Maximising 84
Search Engines
AltaVista 130
Ask Jeeves 136
Basic Searching 132
BBCi 130
Google 129
History 112
MSN Search 129
Results 145
Teoma 137
Using 129
Yahoo 129
Searching
Additional Features 150
Advanced 132, 136
Alternative Terms 136
AND 136
Approaches 105
Basics 132
By Address 106
Crawlers 113
History 112
in Internet Explorer 110
OR 136
Phrases 134
Results 145
Search Terms 133
Spider 113
Today 115
Unwanted Results 135

Index

Secure Connection
  Symbol   10
Security   9
Sites
  Finding   105
Software
  Buying   18

T

Tool Bars
  Move/Remove   85
Toolbar
  Customising   86
Trade Associations   203
TrustUK   203

U

URL
  Components of   106
  Extended   109
Username
  Selecting   41

W

Web Directories
  Conclusions   127
  Google   123
  History   112
  Problems   117
  Yahoo   118
Web Pages
  Headers and Footers
    See Printing
  Page Setup   92
  Print Preview   90
  Printing   89
  Revisiting   68
  Saving   102
Web Site
  Defined   3
  Interacting with   76
  Moving Around   64